T0051722

"Colorado architect Bob West was already half qualified for cowboy life when he bought a Wyoming ranch. He loved vast wild spaces, enjoyed hours on horseback, and had a deep respect for the land, its people, and creatures. The other half—backbreaking labor, a surprising reliance on machinery, gleefully fickle weather, and finances that rarely penciled out—he learned the hard way. Learn he did, and it's a testament to West's spirit that he held on. The take on ranch life in *Twenty Miles of Fence*, written with Janet Fogg, is both unsparing and yet so lyrical as to make readers yearn to give it a try themselves."

—GWEN FLORIO, author of the award-winning Lola Wicks Mystery series

"If you ever doubt that Wyoming is not for the weak, *Twenty Miles of Fence* will dispel you of that notion, with writing so vivid you'll shiver at the January blizzards, smell the fresh-cut summer hay, and hear the river rushing on a cool evening. The reader is treated to an unfiltered look at what real cattle ranching is like, without the romance and legend. Bob West's transformation from greenhorn to a man in tune with the land and animals shows grit and determination much like the landscape itself. This is a true story of homecoming, an unflinching look at the seemingly insurmountable challenges and the ultimate triumph."

—SHANNON BAKER, award-winning author of the Kate Fox Mystery series

TWENTY MILES OF FENCE

Blueprint of a Cowboy

BOB WEST WITH JANET FOGG

UNIVERSITY OF NEBRASKA PRESS   LINCOLN

© 2023 by Bob West and Janet Fogg

All rights reserved

The University of Nebraska Press is part of a land-grant institution with campuses and programs on the past, present, and future homelands of the Pawnee, Ponca, Otoe-Missouria, Omaha, Dakota, Lakota, Kaw, Cheyenne, and Arapaho Peoples, as well as those of the relocated Ho-Chunk, Sac and Fox, and Iowa Peoples.

♾

Library of Congress Cataloging-in-Publication Data
Names: West, Bob (Rancher), author.
Title: Twenty miles of fence: blueprint of a cowboy / Bob West with Janet Fogg.
Description: Lincoln: University of Nebraska Press, [2023] | Includes bibliographical references.
Identifiers: LCCN 2022022445
ISBN 9781496233578 (paperback)
ISBN 9781496235329 (epub)
ISBN 9781496235336 (pdf)
Subjects: LCSH: West, Bob (Rancher) | Cowboys—Wyoming—Biography. | Ranchers—Wyoming—Biography. | Ranch life—Wyoming. | BISAC: BIOGRAPHY & AUTOBIOGRAPHY / Personal Memoirs
Classification: LCC F596 .W483 2023 | DDC 978.7092 [B]—dc23/eng/20220816
LC record available at https://lccn.loc.gov/2022022445

Set and designed in Arno Pro by Mikala R. Kolander.

This book is dedicated to those whose lives and livelihoods are or were entirely dependent upon the land and nature, including all of the Wyoming cowboys and neighbors who so graciously showed me and my family "the best of the West."

I can never walk in the boots of my great-great-grandfather or in those of the tribes whose lives were steered by the seasons, but I do walk the lands where Natives once walked. I hope I step lightly, that what I designed and built, what I created or preserved or nurtured, honors all who have gone before.

—BOB WEST

How do you describe the utter vastness of Wyoming prairie?
The smell? The clarity of the air? The inability to judge distance?
   The solitude.
   Where you can hear the sun set.
   —JANET FOGG

CONTENTS

List of Illustrations   xi

Preface   xiii

Acknowledgments   xv

1. The Bump in the Road   1
2. The Devil's Washtub Ranch   3
3. Two Boys with Sticks   8
4. Our Search   14
5. The Best of Times   27
6. Funeral Music   28
7. Never Buy a Used Bull   31
8. A Bouncing Baby Bull   36
9. Everything's Fine Except My Pride   38
10. Big River, Big Trouble   42
11. Horse Tradin'   49
12. Money Money   58
13. The Meeting   62
14. An Honest-to-God Roundup!   73
15. The Trout Whisperers   79
16. The Sale Barn   83
17. Scours, Scours, Scours   92
18. The Boys from Boulder   100
19. Murphy's Law   113
20. Independence Day!   116
21. Bull Rider   120
22. Feeding Time!   126
23. A Red-Tailed Hawk   132

24. Buffalo Dance   135

25. The Boys from Boulder Return   140

26. The Calf   147

27. Zip   151

28. Midnight Visitor   154

29. Snake Snapping   158

30. The Boy Scout Camp   163

31. Number 72   170

32. Tepee Rings and Tools of Flint   171

33. Boobs!   179

34. Developers   181

35. Change   184

36. Road Trip   186

37. A Blizzard Is Coming   192

38. More Than Fishing   195

39. A Good Life   198

    Afterthoughts   204

    Bibliography   207

ILLUSTRATIONS

1. A curve of the North Laramie River — 4
2. The Devil's Washtub — 6
3. Black angus grazing in tall grass pasture — 26
4. No Trespassing sign with the Devil's Washtub Ranch's brand — 37
5. Sketch noting new structures built on the Devil's Washtub Ranch — 64
6. Upper cabin alongside the North Laramie River — 66
7. Sketch of drinking deck addition to upper cabin — 66
8. Completed drinking deck addition to upper cabin — 67
9. Sketch of vision for the stone smokehouse — 71
10. Stone smokehouse repurposed as a play tower/fort — 71
11. Sorting cattle in the Devil's Washtub Ranch corral expansion — 74
12. Riding Tuff, Bob West herds a steer prior to roping — 105
13. Drag and flank riders during roundup — 107
14. Sketch of branding efforts on the Devil's Washtub Ranch — 109
15. Bob West grabs the rope prior to wrestling a calf to the ground for branding — 111
16. Sketch of new cabin — 121
17. New cabin — 121
18. Bob West removing baling twine from round bale — 130
19. Bob West in tractor, rolling out hay for herd — 131
20. Branding irons ready to be heated — 144
21. The Boy Scout Lodge — 166

PREFACE

I'm a third generation Coloradoan and true westerner at heart. My family two-stepped with the very foundation of historical influences, honing their livelihood and faith against the patterns of western culture and beliefs. Honesty, courage, independence, freedom, and a strong work ethic are the bedrock of this region and its people, and they are my foundation as well.

Everyday life with its acceleration of technology, population pressure, and shift to high-rise living made me, a young urban professional and architect of those actual high-rise structures, challenge my core beliefs. During the early years of my design career, I found myself compromising elements of my own being, including my relationships with those whose hearts beat in the slow, steady rhythm of my own. I questioned my relationship with nature and its raw, unyielding power, and I doubted my basic belief in a higher reason for life, along with my ability to live with what I felt to be the proper respect for life's true meaning.

This book recalls more than a decade of experiences, starting in 1995, when I decided to escape the pretense—the false, half-life I lived—and to become, quite simply, a cowboy. To accomplish this, I, along with my wife, her family, and my best friend, bought a working cattle ranch in Wyoming, away from the bluster and bustle of the Front Range with its all-consuming urban sprawl and the omnipresent noise that accompanies people and their expensive toys.

Little did I know how these years would challenge me, change my life, and bring me back to my true self. I became a cowboy, and my life was saved.

Bob West

ACKNOWLEDGMENTS

I had no idea how demanding it would be to create a book—a narrative encompassing the years I learned how to cowboy on the Devil's Washtub Ranch. Reading my journals and having subsequent discussions with my sons and co-writer Janet prompted unexpected emotions and memories shared within *Twenty Miles of Fence*.

We've been blessed with talented support and would like to thank Richard Fogg, best-selling author, for editing early drafts. Much appreciation to our peer reviewers, Richard Knight, professor emeritus of wildlife preservation at Colorado State University, and Shannon Baker, a two-time Rocky Mountain Fiction Writers Writer of the Year, who so generously shared their knowledge about ranching and writing when evaluating our manuscript.

Working with the exceptional team at the University of Nebraska Press has been an honor. We would especially like to thank our insightful copy editor, Hope Houtwed, and editors Clark Whitehorn and Sara Springsteen, whose support and guidance have been generous and invaluable.

We feel fortunate to have worked with each of you.

TWENTY MILES OF FENCE

1. THE BUMP IN THE ROAD

Wind sluiced around my red Chevy s-10 truck, creating some sort of odd tunnel effect that made the thick, whining sound of the tires against snow-covered asphalt thrum in the cab and resonate in our ears. I increased the speed of the windshield wipers, and I swear I heard a cadence of gulps, that of a freshly caught trout held proudly aloft, gasping for water and finding only thin, unfulfilling air. Already unsettled, an "Open Range" sign riddled with bullet holes caught my eye. Then we were past, on eighteen miles of a one-and-a-half-lane, pot-holed, worn-with-age asphalt roadway—leading from civilization to nowhere.

The snowflakes grew thicker and flew faster, gyrating around my Colorado truck. Tucker and I were engulfed by a white landscape of movement, without any hint of illumination save for the pallid twin beams cast by my truck's headlights.

We chatted nervously about nothing then our conversation faded away, also to nothing.

Even though I knew my new ranch partner and best friend sat beside me, I drove alone. My nervous hands on the cold steering wheel not only fought the power of a Wyoming blizzard but also held the burden of my family's trust, and along with myriad other responsibilities, they yearned to nurture thousands of acres of newly acquired land.

For someone who refused to discuss ending the life of an ancient family pet when it could still gaze at me with hopeful brown eyes, I now held an abundance of life in my hands. Sacred life. Sacrosanct. Romantic perhaps, rather than realistic, especially for someone who planned to raise beef for the market, but my heart would never change. Already my protective streak encompassed every calf and cow, every horse, every hawk and deer and antelope that drank from our river.

What in the hell had I done?

My idea. My responsibility. All of it.

Tucker asked if I knew where we were.

I started at the sound of his voice—might have even grimaced at the solemnity of my thoughts as I thrust them back into hiding. I shook my head.

I didn't say it to Tucker, but I couldn't help but wonder whether our names would be mentioned on the ten o'clock news in a few days, with a somberly dressed news anchor saying, "Two men stranded in Wyoming blizzard found dead . . ." I'd read of this happening to unprepared city slickers more than once, but never thought of myself as naive, let alone foolish. Now I wasn't so sure.

My right foot tapped a nervous jig on the brake pedal as I slowed until we crept along. My compact pickup truck felt like an abandoned toy, not at all tough enough for this vast Wyoming solitude.

Just when I began to think about stopping, the pattern of white inhaled, paused, and with a push of wind that pitched the truck sideways, the snow stopped falling. At that precise moment we hit . . . the bump in the road! I drew in a big breath and slapped the steering wheel.

Over the summer, during one of our due diligence visits, I had entertained my boys on this stretch of road by stomping on the accelerator, pushing my obliging truck to soar over that simple bump in the road. On those sun-filled trips, as we approached the bump, the boys would chant, "Faster, faster!" in anticipation. I always obeyed, and my head would brush the roof liner a moment before my butt rebounded against the seat cushion.

Tonight, butt firmly ensconced, relief warmed me. I felt like laughing as uproariously as my boys but instead found myself grinning into the night.

2. THE DEVIL'S WASHTUB RANCH

Water rights. Fishing rights. Cattle auctions. Horse auctions. Mineral rights. Brand ownership. The cost of hay. The cost of tractors. A new bridge. Collapsing fishing cabins. A new corral. BLM leases. Adjacent property owners. Twenty miles of fence.

We'd studied it all, debated, crunched numbers, debated some more, and shook our heads over the numbers. We were apprehensive. Not just apprehensive, we were scared. Not of the work or learning new skills or of making mistakes. We were afraid of the amount of money we needed. In addition to purchasing the ranch itself, we needed more than a chunk of change to build the property back up to a level of pride, and pride isn't cheap.

The Wheatland Ranch, with 3,200 deeded acres, 620 acres of leased BLM land, and about twenty miles of fence, rode in at three times the size of the other properties we'd considered. But those flat and rocky windswept plains haunted my imagination.

Beneath the stern countenance of nearby Laramie Peak rolled these gentle-seeming foothills of the Front Range, but gentle they weren't. Sliced open by the North Laramie River, a rock-edged canyon meandered between walls of tougher rock, forcing the river into snake-like undulations through the property. Swaybacked buildings and abandoned farm machinery, left in testament to the moment its useful life ended, dotted the landscape, adding a melancholy yearning for what had been, or perhaps what might yet come to be.

So we opened the barn door. As my wife, Katie, and I couldn't afford even the door, let alone a barn, first we escorted her father, Walter, up to the arid plains he'd never before visited. Then her two brothers, Steven and Brian. Californians all, they swiftly grasped the potential of this real

1. A curve of the North Laramie River cutting through the Devil's Washtub Ranch near Wheatland, Wyoming. Courtesy Bob West.

estate play. We knew they enjoyed noteworthy efforts and emphasized that aspect. Walter and Steven, both structural engineers, embraced thorny projects that took years, sometimes even decades, to come to fruition. Brian wore a badge. A Los Angeles police officer, I caught the gleam in his eye when we joked about Wyatt Earp and Marshall Dillon.

Then we took my best friend, Tucker, to the ranch. Amused by his choice of shoes—thin Italian loafers, ostrich leather, I think—I grinned and bit my tongue to forestall my prayer that we wouldn't trip over any rattlesnakes. A fisherman, the two miles of private blue-ribbon trout fishing ignited his curiosity.

After looking at the fishing cabins and the ranch headquarters and the bulls, we hopped over rocks alongside the rush of the North Laramie River. There, I watched in wonder as Tucker transformed. Despite his dapper footwear, his gait changed. He cast off his city-slicker pace—that

THE DEVIL'S WASHTUB RANCH

hurried, narrow, never-look-someone-in-the-eye gait—to stride easily across the open expanse of rock-strewn meadow. Tucker's face and shoulders relaxed. He looked taller and more robust, infinitely more natural, more *himself*, when he unhurriedly shook hands and cracked a joke with Glenn Harrison, the ranch owner. Tucker's age dropped five years, perhaps eight, as he considered the possibility of joining our endeavor.

A cowboy? Why not?

My wife and I drove north again and again.

We discovered tantalizing secrets about this special piece of Wyoming, and our confidence and dedication leaped forward with the grace and speed of the white-tailed deer we repeatedly startled as we tromped around the property.

Artifacts abounded, testaments to the lives that once resided here in harmony with nature. We found flint scrapers, knapped to knife-like sharpness for skinning and scraping buffalo hides. We stumbled across tepee rings, tidy, tell-tale stone circles left intact, used and re-used year after year, centuries ago, when poles and hides were swiftly hoisted high and carefully placed stones weighed down the bottom edges of thick, warm buffalo hide. Once upon a time, standing where we stood, where the wind lifted our hats and the hot, autumn sun bit our shoulders, generations of Native tribes handled those very stones, planning summer and autumn hunts for *tatanka*, their shaggy brown, four-legged staple of life. The ranch's low, rolling hills offered sites for buffalo-skinning camps, and the lush river meadows provided protection from the harsh Wyoming winters and winter grass to feed the tribes' herds of horses.

Despite our rampaging imaginations and excited conversation, we found peace on those quiet afternoons of hiking and sitting by the river, or by the Washtub itself.

A surround of large granite blocks and boulders, with its own private waterfall cascading into a deep green pool, the mist rising from the waters created rainbows that bridged the granite's heights. About thirty

2. Surrounded by granite blocks and boulders, the inscrutable basin known as the Devil's Washtub. Courtesy Bob West.

man-sized mounds of stones circled the rim of the cliffs above, possible remnants of long-ago Native burial spires.

The Devil's Washtub.

A spiritual place.

Turtles calmly sunned themselves, ignoring the fervent efforts of my two young sons as they lobbed rocks high, but not far. Even Little Walter, Katie's first son, who joined us every other weekend, didn't have the strength to startle the mellow creatures. And I refused to lift a hand toward that particular effort. Who knew how old these turtles were, what they'd seen? How many ranchers watered their tired horses here? How many cows lumbered down to that pond, shy calves hiding and tripping between momma's longer legs? How many Natives descended slowly to the edge of the pool, only to pause to gaze up to the heavens before bathing in these deep waters?

THE DEVIL'S WASHTUB RANCH

History surrounded us, permeated our souls. Our lungs breathed in the rich scent of cool humid air, spiked with pine and plain old sweat. I tilted my face to the sun and closed my eyes, as the turtles did when sunning themselves. More than once, in the early 1800s, western frontier explorers such as Francis Parkman likely did the same when first enjoying and then writing about this special place. The Devil's Washtub.

Escaping soaking through the soil or creeping almost invisibly down the grassy ravine, it formed many rocks below another basin, still larger and deeper—but not so cool—a natural bathing-tub and a luxurious refreshment in the intense heat. A noble spring of water not far distant—a great basin of rocks, fringed by soft [ferns?], water like crystal many feet deep, and as cold as ice. (Parkman, *The Journals of Francis Parkman*, 465)

3. TWO BOYS WITH STICKS

Glenn loved to talk. Thank goodness I knew how to listen. As the evening progressed my handwritten notes morphed into the illegible pattern of tumbleweeds skipping across the desert. At about one in the morning, Martha, Glenn's wife, sighed dramatically, stood, and went to bed. I nodded goodnight but didn't stop listening. Or scribbling.

With his rough-hewn Marlboro Man face, Glenn's features gave testament to a lifetime of never-ending Wyoming winds, brutal blizzards, and unforgiving sunshine. Reminding me of tree rings during a draught, I could sense the depths of the worry lines punctuating the corners of his eyes and mouth. Soft-spoken for the most part, he enjoyed his role as patient teacher and storyteller, though he revealed a razor-edged temper more than once.

According to Glenn, we should expect seventy to eighty days of calving in the spring, the time of year I thought of as prime ski season in Colorado. From late February to early May, we would wait and worry and watch the mommas for signs of trouble. But Glenn was just warming up.

Two calves had to be pulled last year.

Most calves were born at daylight.

Pine needles cause abortions during the last trimester.

If the calf's heels were up during birth, that was okay.

I glanced at Tucker. We smiled uneasily and hid behind our sweaty aluminum beer cans, sipping simultaneously. Outside, the wind howled. For a moment, I considered joining in.

New bloodlines would be good to introduce this year, so we'd need two more bulls in the spring.

Turn in the bulls with the herd around the first of June.

Smaller bulls weren't registered.

Colorado stock had to be blood-tested before crossing the state line.

We needed to meet Tom at the feedlot. Introduce ourselves. Tomorrow, maybe.

Liquid protein was okay, but more expensive, and it was hard to make sure each cow received their fair share. Cake was better.

Cake? At $162 per ton, it didn't sound like the devil's food treat that so often graced my sons' birthday parties.

Do the first hay cutting in June. Get it in fast because of storms. We'd need to buy hay, too, as our fields don't produce enough.

The '69 GMC panel truck needed brakes.

The '59 Chevy dump truck needed tires.

The '73 flatbed was for feeding.

We needed a better ranch truck.

We needed tools.

We needed to grade the road.

We needed an equipment barn to shelter tractors with an enclosed shop with a stove.

The elevation at the river was 4,800 feet. Cheyenne had an elevation of 6,000 feet. If there was a cloud cap on Laramie Peak the wind would blow.

He would transfer the hundred-year-old brand after we sold the cows. That would be easiest when we had the bill of sale.

I was afraid to interrupt the steady flow of information but wondered why it was difficult to transfer a brand. We'd already closed on the ranch, and ownership of the brand was part of the deal. But I just nodded and kept taking notes.

At one time, the brand had been in Colorado. A quarter-circle C slash. The C stood for Clay, Glenn's dad.

Oh. Maybe that was it. Perhaps transferring the brand was symbolic of losing his final link to the ranch, his family's legacy.

The fishing cabin leases expired next spring.

Catch and release only, was what he'd offered.

Stocking fish costs upwards of $1,000 per year. Donaldsons. Rainbow steelhead. Montana wild rainbow. Mixed lake and stream.

Huh?

The Farmer's Union.

The neighbors.

The ditches.

Drilling services.

Who might want a job as our ranch hand. What we should pay him.

Vaccinations. Brucellosis and TB.

Keep the water out of the corral.

Needed a new fence at the pasture.

We should visit the church and dance hall in Esterbrook.

Avon skin softener lotion repelled deer flies.

Now there was a segue that screamed for attention. From church to dance hall to repelling deer flies. I suppressed hysterical laughter and chugged my beer. Stopped taking notes. My head and heart pounded with excitement overlaid by a sick, exhausted feeling. Glenn's words swept past me as effortlessly as the evening blizzard had swept past my, as I'd now been told, entirely inadequate red truck. A cough would have toppled me.

I'd known the ranch needed work, and lots of it. But based on Glenn's soliloquy, which now resembled a confession, it seemed every piece of equipment either needed repair or replacement, and every single building needed either replacement or repair. It was too much. I couldn't absorb any more. For someone whose sum experience in life with animals included dogs and a few horses, I'd reached maximum saturation. I allowed my eyelids to droop over my burning eyes. Glenn droned on.

Dealing with the Bureau of Land Management.

Wildfires.

Hunting.

Hikers.

Cutting horses.

Tractors.

Sioux artifacts.

It had to have been after 2:30 a.m. when Martha, royally clad in a long fuzzy robe and matching slippers, swept into the living room and clapped her hands, startling my eyes open and halting Glenn, mid-sentence. She glared at us. We tucked tail and shuffled to bed.

I've never been a morning person, but three and a half hours of sleep later, Tucker and I faced our first test as ranch owners. Spread loosely across the rocky pasture, a herd of cattle stood before us. Most of the snow had been swept away by the wind, which now chilled my neck and ears.

Funny. Those big black cows didn't act like they recognized me as one of their new owners. A few paused mid-chews to roll one eye in our direction, but that was the extent of their interest . . . and respect.

I could see the cows' point of view.

Two boys stumbling around, grunting and waving our arms in the air wouldn't intimidate me, let alone a beast weighing more than five hundred pounds. Where were our horses? The snap of leather against leather? The coils of rope grasped firmly in glove-covered hands, strengthened by years of labor?

Glenn proved immovable on the subject. He said we first needed to learn how to move cows while on our own two feet.

Yep, we need to move the cattle into holding pens. Nope, no horses. Not this morning. Pick out a nice big stick, boys, and follow me.

I grimaced at the cows, at Tucker, at Glenn, at the stick in my hand. I knew how to ride! I'd owned horses for years. Had a beautiful four-stall stable behind my house outside of Boulder. Didn't cowboys always ride feisty cutting horses when they herded cattle? That's what I should be doing—what I wanted to do!

But no.

As it was, it took us two tries to get the herd moving. Those stubborn black angus wanted to soak up the early morning sun and chew.

Holding pens? No thanks! I'm comfortable where I am, thank you very much!

Learning how to say "home boss" didn't really help, either. At least I *think* that's what Glenn said we should murmur as we approached those big black rumps and waved our sticks. To be honest, I'm still not sure.

Glenn also said to always stay on the cow's rear quarter, that we didn't need to touch them with our hands or sticks. Supposedly, when we moved to the right spot, they'd move too.

Or not.

Tucker did learn to stay away from the fence when a couple of cows pivoted adroitly and trotted back toward him, ready to stomp on through. They didn't think twice. Better a flattened Tucker than an immovable fence, right? Glenn saved him, though. Standing inside the gate to the holding pen, he shook the cake he carried in a pail, and the cows swerved as one, trotting to Glenn like hungry cats responding to the sound of a can opener.

"Home boss," my ass.

At that precise moment I realized I could never play poker with that sly, old rancher. His face didn't betray a hint of amusement, even though he knew, and he knew the cows knew, and now we knew, that Glenn could have easily moved that entire herd by himself.

Like the sun rising before us, it swept over me that he'd done it before, many times. After all, Glenn ranched alone. Neither his adopted son nor daughter chose the ranching way. No hired hands. So, he'd trained his cattle to respond to the sound of his cake 'n' pail. Today, he had a couple of boys carrying sticks to help him. If we'd been on horseback, acting cool and cowboy-like, we would have scattered that herd every which way, running off weight and damaging his years of training.

Embarrassed and amused, I waved my stick and muttered "home boss" a few more times. I decided to match his poker face and raise him one. From then on, stubborn would be my middle name. If Glenn wanted me to wave a stick around, so be it. He could even choose the stick. I needed to learn everything I could from him, and he was as much a novice at teaching ranching as I was at learning ranching. But he'd already shown us tinhorns a thing or three.

We counted 107 cows before taking three truckloads to the feedlot. With calves averaging five hundred pounds and prices at about fifty cents per pound, I had the first true glimpse of the financial reality of ranching when Glenn also selected ten old toothless mommas to sell.

Make that the financial *unreality* of ranching.

4. OUR SEARCH

Poised and ready. Stiff new cowboy boots. Chomping at the bit. That would be me, not one of our horses. Before we visited the calm waters of the Devil's Washtub, my enthusiasm for ranching nearly precipitated a disaster when we made an offer for an honest-to-God cattle ranch near Laramie, Wyoming.

We'd spent four years raising the dust of back roads, humming over cattle crossings, opening gates, and closing them carefully behind us. We'd visited dry ranches desiccated into twelve-year-old beef jerky by heat and sun and the ever-present Wyoming winds. We'd oohed and aahed over pristine, overpriced ranches nestled into wide curves of the Laramie River, lush with green grass, outbuildings painted to match with all-blue or all-red metal roofs, houses a perfect white to reflect the summer heat. And we'd scrutinized until cross-eyed our ranch agent's hand-drawn maps—backs of envelopes consumed by Escher-like sketches—while notes about following the asphalt to the third dirt road on the left past the yellow mailbox, then turning onto the left lane at the Y in the road just before the twelve-mile mark, then taking a sharp right after the double cattle guards and following that lane until you reached the dry riverbed where you turn right again rattled through our brains.

Hundreds of miles, possibly thousands, looking at two, three, five properties in a weekend, staying at old motels with roll-to-the-center mattresses, indulging in fast food, with the occasional fabulous steak thrown in when the locals condescended to share their secret restaurants with us, the greenhorn wannabee cowboys from Colorado.

I might have looked the part. Almost. Lean and naturally bowlegged. Tan from years of bicycle racing, squint lines already radiating from the corners of my light-blue eyes. But my wife didn't look or act like a cowgirl; she didn't fit the mold, although her rich-girl ass filled a pair of tight jeans with smooth perfection, and her shoulder-length brown hair flirted and snapped beneath her newest cowboy hat.

We liked horses and owned several, enjoying rides in the evening with our four-year-old son perched in front of me, clutching the saddle horn with his slender fingers, while our oldest son, at six years of age, often sat behind his mother, arms wrapped snug-as-a-bug around her waist for only seconds at a time, before his innate exuberance overwhelmed him, followed by a rapid flapping of arms and hands as he expounded upon some tale. The boys were safe though, even if they sat atop the saddles without us. Our beasts of burden acted more like large domesticated dogs than horses, pampered and sedate in their fancy stable behind our house on five acres, east of Boulder.

We wanted more and I precipitated that want.

I'd grown jaded by my high-stress, principal-in-charge career. Negotiating contract language and holding my clients' hands as they negotiated financing no longer made my top ten list of joys. Never had, really. But when attorneys from California hitchhiked across the Nation, architecture changed. Now, design decisions were compromised by wrangling insurers or less-than-honorable contractors, but primarily by developers who conveniently forgot at bill-paying time that our firm wasn't a bank before depositing their multiple millions of profits at the end of the day.

The dream of a ranch and spending more time with my family sustained me through evening meetings with planning boards, presentations to city councils, coordinating a huge design and construction team from concept through construction administration, all the while coping with thousands of emails and an occasional rancorous phone call. And that just touched on the project side of the profession. Along with several partners I also managed the firm, from marketing to human resources to analyzing financial statements to mentoring young designers. We coped with all of it and did it well, but building a haven with my wife where we could be real people, not the perception of someone else, kept me laughing and sane.

Only hesitantly had I whispered my secret dream to Katie so many years before, but she hadn't let me down. This woman I adored, she wanted what I wanted. But first we had to find the right property. The right size, in the right condition, a few hours from Boulder, and one we could afford. We were both particular when it came to land and location.

Despite the abundance of her father's money, Katie knew how to work as hard as I did, and she also knew real estate. Together, we'd developed several projects, and before our marriage she'd purchased and managed buildings for her family.

Hand-in-hand we set out on my quest, now become our quest.

Searching for the perfect ranch is complicated and time-consuming. First there's the extensive travel. Miles on the road, from interstate to state highways, then lesser, one-lane dirt roads throughout our western states. Arguments over fence lines, water rights, and actual property ownership of advertised land plague optimistic and unsuspecting buyers used to purchasing quarter-acre platted suburban homes. We had a couple of edges, including knowledge of real estate development and architectural design, but our "ace in the hole" turned out to be one of the best ranch real estate agents in the wild, wild West, Bill White.

Around sixty years old, Bill looked the part, with his white Stetson cowboy hat, stained gray by sweat as silent testament to his cattle ranching experience. He'd managed the acquisition and sale of ranches for Hollywood notables, including James Arness, also known as Marshall Matt Dillon of the long-running *Gunsmoke* series. Over the years Bill had also owned cowboy bars, including the Campus Lounge in Denver and the historic Saratoga Inn in Wyoming.

One of our goals was to keep the distance from our house in Boulder at a minimum since the ranch was going to be a weekend retreat. With our "day jobs" and our boys' schooling and extracurricular activities, we had to keep the travel radius below three hours. Our wish list included water, fishing opportunities, and possibly enough acreage to run cattle, though we had zero experience with raising beef. Besides fairly close proximity, another absolute was to find a place to ride our horses, as we had outgrown our backyard corral and neighborhood trails.

Early in our search, we stumbled on the perfect, newly-on-the-market ranch on the eastern slope of one of the Spanish Peaks near Trinidad when my wife mentioned our quest to a college friend who happened to be representing the sellers.

South on I-25 we motored through the megalopolises of Denver, Colorado Springs, and Pueblo, to the Aguilar exit. Smooth, well-maintained asphalt morphed into cracked old asphalt then into dusty dirt roads through the Spanish-influenced town. As we slowed, I opened my window. With too many boarded-up 1894-vintage stone buildings, the smell of memories, of heat from rusting tin roofs, and of desiccated wood squatted over the main street; this worn downtown had no doubt hosted its share of gunfights. With the image of the true West shadowing us, on we drove to the literal end of the road.

As we rounded the last bend, I hit the brakes. Hard. We had to have taken a wrong turn.

A leather-faced gentleman that I could best describe as a seventy-five-year-old cousin to Pancho Villa, including cross belts of ammunition wrapped diagonally across his chest and back, stood in the middle of the road. But it was the lever action rifle he cradled so casually in his arms and the shiny pair of six-guns strapped to his hips that accelerated my heart.

What the hell?

I glanced at my boys in the backseat. I'd never seen their eyes so large. Katie and I exchanged one long look as I slowly finished rolling down my window. The man stalked over to rest one work-worn hand on my door as he leaned down and in.

I cleared my throat and stuttered something along the lines of, "We're meeting a real estate agent to look at your neighbor's ranch, maybe wanting to buy it."

His brown eyes softened. A slight smile deepened some of the wrinkles around his eyes, and he leaned in farther to wave at my shaken boys. "Hola. I'm Pedro. Guess I might be your neighbor, then." He straightened and waved ahead. "Go on in," he finished as he backed away so we could proceed.

After getting over the initial shock, I accelerated slowly to avoid enveloping our potential neighbor in a cloud of dust. We shared nervous laughter about having an armed guard at the ranch entrance not being such a bad thing, especially with it being such a remote location.

Soon, a 635-acre mountain valley captured our attention. Surrounded by thousands of acres of Federal wilderness, this ranch and the adjacent one had to block most of the access to those pristine, government-owned acres. No wonder our potential neighbor tried to frighten possible trespassers.

Built in the early 1900s, the two-story house needed repair, though the stone well house dug into the side of an embankment had weathered the years. The meadow of thick waist-high grasses and wildflowers climbed the valley edges, stopped only by the old-growth forest. Aspen and fir trees sporting thirty-inch diameter trunks marched sedately up the low mountain slopes. A small, year-round brook punctuated by a stock pond near the edge of the meadow provided water for livestock, and probably deer and big cats.

It was perfect, exactly what we'd envisioned, and offered at a reasonable price. We immediately signed an offer.

Our dream turned into a nightmare when the title work arrived.

A document that should have been a few pages summarizing a title company's historical research about the ranch landed on our porch with a thump. A one-inch-thick summary of bad news. Somewhere around 1875, the original ranch owner sold the timber rights, mineral rights, grazing rights, and water rights for the ungodly sum of one dollar to a man with the last name of "Smith." In retrospect we should have closed our eyes and bought the place, but my wife's father and his accountants and lawyers were dead set against it. They and we knew that descendants of "Smith" could someday descend upon the valley to claim their rights, leaving barren acreage divested of timber, water, and who knows what minerals.

Unlikely? Perhaps. Probably. But a risk nevertheless.

We withdrew our offer.

Future weekend road trips included outings to remote hideaways in Rye, the Cuchara Valley, La Veta, and Westcliffe, all beautiful in their own right, but we'd been tainted by seeing the best ranch, first. None of the successors kindled desire, compounded by rising prices and fast sales. Texas, historically thirsty for vacation property, had emerged from its oil and gas recession, and Texans had money to spend. We'd missed our southern Colorado opportunity and redirected our gazes north, to Wyoming.

Choked by too many dusty roads and drowned by water rights issues, disappointment threatened our efforts. It took my own quiet brand of stubbornness to hold our quest together. I could still envision a future when we would strap saddles atop alert cutting horses and herd black angus across the open range. I would stop driving a lumbering van and instead saddle up a beautiful white-and-chestnut horse. And with my consuming day job gnawing off chunks of my joy and spitting out my work ethic, I literally counted the minutes, ready to fulfill my dream with those I loved best, even if I could only live that dream part-time, on the weekends.

I yearned to teach the boys to fly fish, to respect nature, to ride and shoot, and, most importantly, to appreciate the sweat of a job well done. They were exuberant and funny and spoiled—typical great kids—and I would teach them as I'd been taught by my father, by working side-by-side, no matter how large the chore. We would build fences; they could hand me nails. We would listen to meadowlarks sing while chopping wood or cleaning saddles or barbecuing ribs. Together, we would learn to rope and brand and how to feed cattle and watch with wonder as day-old calves sucked at their momma's teats. To work and play and live without the buzz of humanity all around us, without TV or VCRs or the constant harangue of video games pinging in the background. The rich, subdued sounds of nature would sing us to sleep beneath billions of stars unspoiled by city lights.

Swayed by the pristine beauty of acreage near Laramie and hungry to close on our own property, Katie and I tuned out the warnings of our curmudgeon of a ranch agent, Bill, who'd heard that mosquitoes could be quite a problem in that particular location. We shrugged and said we could spray if there were mosquitoes. There were mosquitoes in Colorado too.

Bill narrowed his eyes and I think he mentally spat a bad taste from his mouth before continuing his worrywart words. It seemed there was a toad—an endangered species no less—that might just hop and croak on our proposed purchase. The University of Wyoming studied this toad and the areas it inhabited, which might restrict our ability to build. But we didn't care about toads either. Instead, we joked about what toads ate for breakfast, lunch, and dinner. Mosquitoes! If the toad inhabited our property, perfect. We'd have our own, built-in mosquito control. The boys laughed hysterically at this joke. Bill shrugged and scheduled our closing.

A few days before that long-anticipated date, Katie drove north alone, for one last look at the Laramie property. A final walk-through, so to speak, though walking a thousand acres would literally take weeks and she only planned a quick trip—a balmy spring afternoon drive, a walk through the house and primary barn to refresh her memory, dip a toe in the river to gauge the water level, then steer the van south toward home again.

In a panic, she called me at the office.

"You have to get up here right now!" my wife demanded. But she wouldn't tell me why, though I insisted that she first reassure me she was fine, which she did. But she refused to explain further.

I couldn't help but envision the Lone Ranger vaulting onto Silver's back as I plunged into my truck. I didn't cut quite the same romantic image in a well-used red truck with its cracked windshield, but I knew my dedication to rescuing my damsel in distress was equal to the Ranger's most daring of escapades.

I galloped north.

Late afternoon, as I skidded around the last bend on the dirt road before entering what would soon be our property, I saw the neighbor had a new dark gray horse in his corral, a nervous horse, stomping and tapping his hooves into the dirt. With the swish of his tail and a shiver of his hide, that horse's hide blanched into dappled gray. I mimicked his nervous dance to flatten my brake pedal with both feet, raising a cloud of dust to engulf my truck. I squinted through the airborne grit. Covered by innumerable mosquitoes, that miserable horse made every inch of my body itch.

Trying to swallow the sour in my throat and stomach, I eased my feet off the brake pedal and reluctantly followed the dirt road onto our soon-to-be ranch, our haven, the beautiful property we'd chosen so excitedly after four long years.

Standing next to the ranch house, Katie proved to be the proverbial vision in white, clad in full mosquito regalia, including swathes of netting around her face and neck. I pulled the truck close, stepped out, and the oily, decidedly unromantic scent of Cutters wafted over to kiss me. Not what she'd worn on our wedding day. We looked at one another, shook our heads, shook the ranch owner's agent's hand in farewell, apologized to him, and high-tailed it back to Boulder.

Depressed.

Disconsolate.

Describe the color blue and we wallowed in it.

The very next Saturday morning, though, found us sweet-talking our sons into the minivan for one final weekend hunt with Bill. Tan and squint-eyed from too much sun, he walked like a cowboy and talked like a cowboy—what I wanted to be. Honest and blunt, always. He'd warned us off the mosquito ranch and now I trusted him even more. He didn't rub it in. In fact, he never mentioned it again.

But the mosquito ranch took a walloping bite out of our hope, leaving us in absolute accord; out of respect, we would spend the day with Bill, but if we didn't like this next property, our quest ended. Our sons wanted to wrestle or go swimming or play T-ball with their friends instead of sitting in the backseat for yet another road trip. They didn't understand, but we felt we owed Bill this last weekend, this final opportunity.

It seemed Bill had heard about a ranch near Lusk, Wyoming, that he thought we might like. He hadn't seen it himself, but he'd heard good things. As was often the case, he would meet us at the property. Since Katie and I had essentially given up, we didn't really listen to his description of the land or the buildings, what was included or not, but we dutifully noted his directions. Pessimistic? Yep.

Four and a half hours of a cooped up, seat-belted, air-conditioned drive north on sticky asphalt highway ensued. Worse yet, our sons smelled our lack of enthusiasm and reached unfamiliar levels of discord, alternately whining and squabbling with generous handfuls of are-we-there-yet thrown in.

Finally at the ranch house, we tumbled from the van to stretch the kinks out of our assorted limbs. Even to our jaded eyes the property did look kind of promising.

Trailed by Bill and two yawning, yellow ranch dogs, the ranch owner trotted energetically across the wide porch to greet us. But rather than offering me his howdy along with an outstretched hand, the rancher reached into a back pocket, went down on one knee, and tugged loose something that reflected the midday sun. Swiftly, he pointed it at my boys.

Insect repellent.

A can of insect repellent versus armies of newly hatched horseflies. Whoa, could they bite!

We chased the boys back into the van.

As I belted myself in, Bill leaned heavily against my door, forestalling our escape. I rolled down the glass and rolled my eyes up at him. He ignored my expression and settled more thoroughly against the van. I felt it sway sideways.

It seemed there was a ranch near Wheatland, two hours south of Lusk, two hours closer to home. Right on our way, in fact. A not really for-sale ranch, not yet anyway. But Bill had heard rumors these past weeks. After a lifetime of brutally hard work, of bad luck seasoned generously with barely-scraping-by income, cattle prices at rock bottom, a recent mild heart attack, and neither son nor daughter interested in following in his boot steps, that second-generation Wheatland rancher recently confessed to his fellow ranchers, his friends at the café, that he'd had enough.

Katie and I sighed in a soft duet of weariness, but we nodded and agreed to meet Bill in Wheatland. It was on the way home, and we'd need to stop in a couple of hours anyway so the boys could run laps around the van while we doled out sodas and sandwiches.

We made pretty good four-lane interstate time, pulling into the parking lot of "the" coffee shop—the Wheatland Inn—in a drab little town lined with sunbaked streets and more pickup trucks than cars, to meet Bill at about 5:30 p.m. Katie slipped into the back seat to sit with the boys, so Bill stepped into the front cab, followed by a tanned, rawhide strip of a man, a cowboy dressed in dusty jeans and a cotton snap-down cowboy shirt, faded from too many washings. We shook hands in front of Bill's face.

Lee, now a ranch broker like Bill, spent the first seventy years of his life on horseback. Here sat a cowboy. He didn't belong in my minivan any more than a brilliant-eyed hawk belonged in a cage. Face furrowed from squinting into the sun, the palm of his hand felt as tough as the stirrups strapped to my saddle back home. He exuded the scent of piñon sap and dusty sage, countless cups of coffee, sweat produced by muscle-tearing days of work, and the silent confidence gained from a lifetime of gazing over vast horizons.

Betrayed by his white forehead, where his grimy and creased straw cowboy hat usually shaded his eyes from the sun, his worn-at-the-heels cowboy boots, smoothed by a decade of heels skidding across corrals to wrestle down a half-wild roped calf that didn't really want to be branded, this man would never shed his cowboy ways. More importantly for us, Lee knew the Wheatland ranch owner and had discussed selling the ranch for him.

We traveled for about thirty minutes on a weed-choked two-lane asphalt road, curling around to the north of town and then west, passing strafed road signs telling tales of the bored cowboys who'd taken potshots at the immobile targets. Asphalt gave way to gravel and then dirt, and as we passed a huge, tilted mailbox guarded by a half dozen slumbering black angus, Bill announced we'd entered the ranch property.

Soured by disagreeable first impressions, only my respect for Bill kept me from turning around. He sensed my rebellion and acted on it when he pulled a cassette tape from his shirt pocket and popped it into the player. The theme song from *Bonanza*, the iconic 1960s television series, engulfed us. Laughing, I drove on, as Katie and the boys chortled in the back seat.

High prairie surrounded us. Rocky and rough, tinder-dry tufts of grass interrupted by an occasional cactus. The road, mostly stiff ruts, desperately needed grading. Every rusted metal gate moaned in protest when opened and complained even more vociferously when closed. The land itself seemed dog-eared and wrung-out, incapable of creating or sustaining new life.

Frowning, I looked around carefully, but despite the thumpity-thump of the energetic music, my off-putting impressions of a bedraggled and tired property remained.

The theme song ended, changing into the deep, melodious moos of cows calling for their calves.

I drove another mile or so then braked abruptly to a stop, two-footing the pedal. A new habit, it seemed. But the view *made* me stop; it deserved a moment of respect.

Below us, but not too far below, the North Laramie River meandered through a lush green meadow. Though we couldn't hear the chuckling water, it sparkled and frothed against curves and bends, slipping from sun into shadow where the toes of thick pine trees and downy cotton-woods reached greedily for snowmelt. A tumble of glacial boulders interrupted the trees, but tall grass swayed in gentle persuasion against the smooth gray rock, parting to reveal deep pockets of icy cold water where trout played hide 'n' seek with the sun. In the distance, the snow-capped pinnacle of Laramie Peak stretched to the heights, challenging the deep-blue evening sky.

My heart quickened.

3. Black angus grazing in tall grass pasture on the Devil's Washtub Ranch. Courtesy Bob West.

5. THE BEST OF TIMES

I hadn't slept much, and this morning, on the drive north from Boulder to Wheatland, those exit signs looked as enticing to me as a cold beer after a sweat-soaked day working in the sun. I studied the asphalt carefully, wondering if I should ease off the highway. Cruising at a comfortable eighty miles per hour on I-25, we hadn't yet reached the wide-open spaces near the Colorado-Wyoming border. It would be hell easy to choose an exit, any exit, turn the truck around, and head home.

Could I do that? Would I?

Nerves.

After so many miles and so many disappointments, today, our quest would end.

I pressed my lips together and my boot on the gas pedal, increasing our speed to eighty-five miles per hour.

The Harrison Ranch. At 1:00 p.m. it would be ours.

Twenty miles of fence, 3,200 deeded acres, 134 head of black angus cattle plus 20 heifers from this year's crop, two and a half miles of the Laramie River, and what would become for me the very best of times.

6. FUNERAL MUSIC

Empty but neatly labeled in blue marker, a banker's box squatted on the floor between Glenn and Martha. RANCH SALE, the lid said. Simple words to sum up decades of bitter-cold February mornings and sweet, starry August nights. Could that store-bought cardboard contain the terrifying scent of wildfire following months of drought, the joy of a simple picnic supper, fried chicken, potato salad, and sweet tea, laid out atop a striped blanket on a tranquil Sunday afternoon?

Would the memory of Glenn's father, Clay, buried on the ranch, fit in one corner? What about thousands of cattle, born but now gone? Would their bawling, butts-to-the-wind shadows rest easily atop a closet shelf? What of the scattered reminders of Natives and the great herds of buffalo that once grumbled across the hills? Would they acquiesce and go quietly?

Imagining seasons of defeat boxed up alongside moments of exquisite rapture hollowed out my stomach, made my heart ache for the Harrisons and his family before. But that hurt kept getting shoved sideways by my own elation, tinged with nervous anticipation.

The Harrisons' emotions had to be knotted and tangled more than mine. Today, that gnarled old couple was selling their ranch, their livelihood for over sixty years, their home. A reprieve, we'd heard whispered. Stone cold broke, the unkind said aloud. Martha and Glenn planned to build a new house in Wheatland. And this holiday season they would be able to buy a turkey for Thanksgiving dinner, and more, which yesterday might not have been possible.

We penned a six-digit check at the closing, with a gulp and grit your teeth follow-up act, when we signed on the dotted line for a similar amount of new debt.

Note payable in hand, I paused for a moment to envision the old foundation nestled snug in a curve of the river, now *our* river. That concrete whispered regularly to me of logs and leather and broad porches sheltering a dozen or so rough chairs. My fingers itched to start schematic design, but I held off. It would be at least a few years before that foundation could host our new cabin. Instead, first on our agenda? The care and feeding of cattle. Glenn would help. He'd teach us as much as he could stand, as often as we could stand being taught.

Faded Remington prints, cowboys and Indians and cowboys and cattle, observed our proceedings from the walls of the unpretentious Wheatland conference room, and a sweat-stained cowboy hat—upside down, of course, to protect the brim—sat atop the table alongside the stacks of sliding paperwork and multitude of pens. Cowboy country. For real. Real money. Real cows. And a couple of tinhorn cowboys.

Wyoming tough, Martha stopped mid-signature to make light of the deed before her. She grinned and asked Bill if he had any funeral music. No trumpeting marches for the Harrisons' retreat into town; instead, something sweet and sad, in a minor key, please.

I realized then that I'd misjudged the demeanor of those who sat around the table. Rather than anxiety on the part of Bill or Lee, or the notary or attorney or fishing-cabin renter, the uncomfortable postures and stilted conversations revealed a show of respect for the pair of old ranchers for whom life would now change so dramatically. I could see it clearly now. The somber-eyed deference offered up to your elders at family reunions.

Those 3,200 Wyoming acres had nearly consumed Glenn and Martha. Every bit of human energy, ingenuity, and old-fashioned fortitude had been needed to keep their property afloat, especially these last few years. Those struggles impacted us. We'd purchased a ranch with decrepit working equipment, an ancient cowherd seriously in need of shots and other postponed veterinary duties, and sixty years of junk littering the otherwise pristine and unspoiled acres.

But in some quiet, stubborn fashion, the challenge of deciphering and mending and rebuilding sparked an inner core that burned brighter each moment. I had an unyielding outlook toward taking care of what I earned, what I loved, or whatever I took responsibility for. I had a family to support and a ranch to rebuild. What could be better than that?

7. NEVER BUY A USED BULL

Passing through towns with historic names such as Cheyenne and Chugwater, I drove up alone for a crash course in ranching, if alone counts Glenn, me, a hundred and sixty cows, and my little bitty toy truck. Still hadn't replaced it and wasn't sure I would. As I steered past the ranch's tilted solid-steel mailbox, I wondered whether a demolition derby awaited me. I knew that if it came to a physical confrontation, the cows would win. Bashed in hood? Dented door? Broken shocks? Hopefully not, but I'd discovered a weight and a rhythm to caring for this Wyoming land of mine, for nurturing life on lonely, thick-skinned acres, though I'd barely started to hear the opening cadence, let alone hum along.

I picked up Glenn at the main ranch house, headquarters as we liked to call it, and we headed out. As my truck heaved across the knuckles of rock jutting out of the road, Glenn began his morning lessons.

Never buy a used bull. Only virgins.

I didn't dare look at him. Only virgins? Seriously? He said we'd need three this spring. Virgins, that is. How in the hell could you tell whether a bull was a virgin? But I couldn't make myself ask, and he didn't explain.

He harrumphed and I glanced his way as he smoothed his chin with his palm before tilting back his hat. More bull. I could see it coming.

But after we buy 'em, we ask the seller to keep those eating machines 'til May 15th or so. That way, we don't feed 'em.

Ah. That was the second lesson he wanted to share. How to save a few pennies, Glenn style.

We came upon Number 116 and I stopped the truck. We stepped out of the cab to look her over. She sidled away from Glenn, but not too far, and with her dry-blood-coated hind end claiming most of my attention,

I probably imagined the sad look in her eyes. She'd aborted on Thursday and Glenn didn't know why. Maybe from chewing on pine needles. The only good news? Coyotes had cleaned up the remains of her calf. We didn't have to dig a deep hole to bury what was left. Another Glenn-ism. *Always carry a shovel, either to bury something or to lop off the head of a rattlesnake.*

Something? What kind of something? I didn't ask.

Glenn seemed satisfied with 116's health, so we moved on.

Minutes later, my heart nearly galloped out of my chest when I spotted a rifle-toting man striding across the pasture. Shit. I could handle a rifle, but I didn't have one with me. This I didn't expect. My pasture. My ranch. A man with a rifle. I slowed the truck and kept heading his way.

We pulled to a stop and Glenn rolled down his window, stuck his head and arm out, to laugh and wave.

Jim White. A hunter.

Jim carefully kept his rifle pointed to the ground as Glenn introduced us, and Jim proceeded to extol the pleasures of hunting coyotes; said he'd take me out, show me where they denned.

Apparently, Glenn always invited him onto the ranch to hunt coyotes prior to calving season, along with another pair of men from Denver.

I didn't want hunters on our ranch. Period. Yellow-eyed packs of coyotes had lived on this land longer than man, and Jim enjoyed taking aim and spitting death. Not going to happen. Not anymore. Not after this season.

Glenn must have seen the stubborn set of my shoulders, as he then proceeded to tell me, in blood-red detail, how coyotes would snap at the legs of a calf or sick steer and drag it down, shred their belly, and eat their guts while the angus groaned and kicked, still alive.

I didn't argue. It seemed to me that if we wanted the pack to take care of aborted calves and afterbirth, along with deer too old to survive the winter, then we should leave the coyotes alone. Arguing the point now wouldn't work. Glenn had already welcomed Jim to the ranch, and I didn't want to embarrass either man by arguing the point. Next year would be different. I frowned but remained silent as Glenn launched into a lecture on rifles and calibers and who sold the cheapest ammo.

We nodded farewell to Jim and rolled on across the flats. Not too far away, thirty or so antelope grazed in the tall grass. I eased the truck to a stop and the solemn herd stood sentinel, gazing at us for the longest time. Then, without a sound or signal, necks stretched long, they twisted upward as one, as a puff of wind dislodged the dried seeds of a dandelion to soar high over the grass.

A few days later I was reminded again how coyotes have a bad rap in the West.

My awareness of that negative innuendo started in my childhood, with the cartoon adventures of Wile E. Coyote and the Road Runner. Wile E. never won. Ever. Whether blown up by dynamite or slamming face-first into a fake tunnel drawn on a mountain of granite, that tenacious cartoon coyote always lost.

I like to think I have an open mind regarding coyotes. Musical, swift, canny, as long as they didn't bother me or mine, why should we bother them?

Early one Saturday morning the pair of hunters from Denver shot and killed a small female coyote whose rib-jutting thin body looked malnourished. Probably no more than a year old, she wasn't wise or experienced enough to ignore the coyote calls from these supposedly adept hunters.

Chests puffed with pride in their accomplishment, the dynamic duo proclaimed they'd get $25 for her scruffy pelt. Unable to conjure up a single word of praise, I turned my back on them and walked away.

Glenn later told me that the coyote got her revenge. While the pair hunted unsuccessfully for a few more days, the small female's body ripened into a stink-pot, so potent they didn't even want her pelt. A swift burial punctuated the end of their stay.

A wasted death, except that it reinforced my resolve to discourage hunting on our property.

I believe one of the reasons to have a ranch is to learn how to partner with Ma Nature, whether furious, friendly, or benign. Every rancher and cowboy I spoke to hated coyotes and would shoot one without pause. Ranchers interested in serious predator control even hired airplanes as moveable shooting platforms—fixed-wing types, often yellow, much like crop dusters.

Coyotes have a defined territory, with an older experienced male leading a pack of females. This keeps the population somewhat under control. Airplane hunting damages that natural balance, as the older male will try to protect his pack and is frequently killed because of that courage. Another inhumane coyote eradication method uses tainted or rotted meat attached to a small explosive. A rather sickening way to control the critters, and more often than not, a family pet or ranch dog ended up as the victim.

With the demise of the leader of the pack, young males invade a pack's territory and mate uncontrollably, splitting the pack into smaller family units which creates more coyotes. Talk about an ass-backward result.

Nothing conjures an image of the West better than a serenade of coyotes against a midnight sky.

Early morning horseback rides were often escorted by the elongated shadow of a single coyote loping alongside. Always inquisitive, and only threatening when hunting in packs, the lone coyote would often be diverted by a mouse or rabbit, and we would lose our riding companion.

True, we kept a lookout during calving, but even then, I saw the coyotes wait until a momma cow gave birth before swooping in to snatch up the afterbirth and lope away with their messy vitamin-rich meal.

Our future on the ranch would include the loss of calves to lightning strikes, cattle rustlers traveling onto the pasture in a custom-built slaughterhouse on wheels, big cats, and yes, coyotes. Over the course of some two thousand births, we'd only lost *one* to a pack of coyotes. In that particular instance, a young mother cow sadly chose to calve too close to a barbwire fence in a remote part of the ranch. Bloody tracks in the snow evidenced the birth, and the coyotes pulled the calf under the fence before momma could recover her wits. Even if she'd kicked instinctively to protect her newborn, the fence thwarted her efforts.

At the time, the idea of rustlers alarmed me far more than whatever Ma Nature might throw our way. The idea of rustlers slaughtering a momma cow, stealing the beef, and leaving leftover cow parts strewn across the pasture next to a trembling calf, enraged me. More than once, I dreamed of catching one of those folks and engaging in a bit of rangeland justice. Despite cowboy tradition I couldn't help but wonder if the real varmint hadn't been misidentified. I'd call him a modern-day cattle rustler.

8. A BOUNCING BABY BULL

After a long week of long days at the architectural office, the three-hour drive up to the ranch resembled a hiccup. Or more appropriately, a sigh of relief. Yes, I'd become nervous about effectively fulfilling my duties this weekend, but stepping out of the truck onto the wide-open acres eased the hunched-over-a-drawing-board tension in my shoulders. I had a passion for design and knew how to nurture a building from concept until it stretched tall above a solid foundation. Sadly, architecture had morphed into hours on the phone, hours in meetings, hours with planners, and hours managing staff and budgets. What I'd envisioned in my youth came to fruition early in my career. The weight of coordinating a thousand tasks and hours squeezed the satisfaction I derived from design into the back corner.

Along with the Wyoming border came wind. No surprise and I'd never really minded it, not until recently. Now at night I couldn't sleep well if it gusted over fifteen or twenty miles per hour, not in the tin can of a trailer we'd hauled up to use as temporary housing. I couldn't wait for the fishing shack leases to expire so I could move into a cabin with almost-solid walls; then Katie and the boys would join me more often.

I told Glenn I'd take the early shift. Easy enough, what with the subzero wind infiltrating every riveted seam, plus one entire trailer wall drumming in and out. 3:00 a.m.? No problem. Time to nursemaid the heifers.

Calm, bright eyes gleamed at me as I paced through the barn. Eight mommas and two calves. A quiet nursery. When I went out again at 5:30 a.m., a bouncing baby bull greeted me. Just as Glenn warned, the heifers frequently calved in the wee hours of the morning. Now I had proof. New life nestled at my feet.

That minutes-old critter energized me. I checked the whole herd, fed

4. No Trespassing sign with the Devil's Washtub Ranch's brand on the lower corners. Courtesy Bob West.

the cows, and drove the tractor out to spread hay with the hay roller—for the second time. Just as when I'd seen the herd of antelope, I let myself pause in my labors mid-morning when I spotted ten white-tailed deer near the upper basin. I recognized the hypocrisy of raising beef and enjoying steak dinner while remaining anti-hunting. But I simply didn't get it. How could someone shoot an elegant, gentle doe?

The glimpse of a mountain lion, bear, eagle, or hawk always made my heart soar, though depending on proximity, it might also be racing. In truth, my fondness for our less ferocious resident wildlife increased with every sighting. Coyote, deer, antelope, owls, muskrats, river otters, beavers—they called this land home.

I suspected it would be a different story if I needed to hunt to put food on the table, but the bounding-away hind ends of the deer reminded me of my earlier vow. There would be no hunting on my land. As if in affirmation, an eagle cried out from the heights. The remnants of office stress fell from my shoulders.

9. EVERYTHING'S FINE EXCEPT MY PRIDE

The disparity between my "civilized" life in Boulder, a liberal bastion of yuppie types, and cowboy-country Wheatland, with its conservative small-town atmosphere, always enlightened, sometimes entertained, and always provoked thoughts.

From the mind-numbing city council meetings where rich NIMBYs pontificated about protecting prairie dogs to misguided university students fighting to keep dirty, tattered couches on their front porches, Boulder hosted transitory and vocal homeowners from both coasts. They jogged and skied. Rode bicycles on bike paths—or in the middle of the traffic lane—unconcerned about blocking commuters in cars. Picnicked on tables set amid acres of open space land. Purchased organic groceries and hiked in the mountains. Embraced bizarre unworkable rules fashionable for the time. A good, though clearly spoiled life in a striking setting against the foothills. I'd enjoyed this life for a long time, knew it well, and loved many aspects of it. But you had to have money and liberal political beliefs to truly savor life in Boulder.

Life in Wheatland circled around a sometimes brutal physical world, where exercise came in the form of chores and organic vegetables came from your own garden, beef from your own land. Livings were eked out by generations of families that revered *and* cursed Ma Nature, sometimes winning the battles against her but never ending the war.

Arriving at the ranch on a Friday night during calving season did not deliver a gentle transition. We essentially had to switch from a white-collar focus to Carhartt brown—fast—to lessen the risk of injury not only for ourselves but for the animals in our care.

I rolled in late, unloaded my gear, and walked up to the ranch house that Glenn and Martha continued to occupy. They had promised to move when we hired a ranch manager, as long as that didn't happen before completion of their new home in town.

Glenn already had one leg thrust into his insulated Carhartts when Martha opened the door. No time to chat, not this evening. We had a heifer in trouble. I didn't know what kind of trouble, but I suspect the whites of my eyes might have shown when Martha handed her husband several pairs of long, clear plastic gloves.

Cowboy training 101.

We walked down to the calving barn, a small concrete-block building with a metal roof snugged atop an open area enclosing two holding stalls. A steel-railed corral claimed one corner of the open area, along with a steel head catch. I'd briefly looked over this medieval-looking device and thought I understood how it worked.

When closed, and with the cow's body aligned correctly, steel caught the cow around the neck while holding the body steady. Without that head catch, our half-wild open-range cows could and would morph into spinning half-ton demons.

Sprawled haphazardly across the straw-strewn ground, the troubled heifer reminded me of a panting dog after a long run. Glenn paced quietly toward the cow, and she staggered to her feet. Despite her suffering, she remained skittish. With me on one side and Glenn on the other, we eased her past the pivoting gate into the metal stall. With an awe-inspiring bang and shudder, the heifer hit the head catch. One swift pull of a lever and Glenn captured her head.

Stepping carefully around her hind legs, Glenn moved to the back of the cow. I nodded. That girl could still kick.

Glenn tugged those long plastic gloves up past his elbows. He eased one hand into the heifer and murmured that he would first check on the calf's position to see if its head and front legs pointed out. If not, he would need to reach into the cow's womb and turn the calf to the correct position while keeping the cord from wrapping around the calf's neck.

I silently thanked God when Glenn murmured the legs were aligned correctly. Heels up would have meant a breech calf. With a quick, silent belch, my sour stomach settled. Temporarily.

Glenn said we needed to pull the calf or we'd lose the momma, so I grabbed the end of a chain that had been coiled onto a lever mounted on the wall behind us. Glenn carefully looped the end of the chain around the calf's now exposed hocks.

I ground my teeth as we tightened the crank. Too much pressure would strip the hooves off the legs of the tender calf. The calf's legs inched out as momma groaned. Glenn screwed the crank tighter and first the calf's nose, then head slid out. Momma shivered. One last half crank and the calf slid out with a liquid slurp, dropping toward the straw-covered floor.

Glenn caught the calf and eased it down while yelling at me to release the cow from the catch. She'd lost her feet and was being choked to death. I lurched away to stare at multiple levers, not knowing which one to pull.

The poor heifer's eyes bulged out from the pressure around her neck and the weight of her body as I grabbed and pulled on every lever. Finally, the catch opened and the cow flopped sideways onto the straw-covered dirt. She shuddered and sucked in breath after breath. So did I.

I staggered back to look at the calf. Glenn told me to grab the back hooves and lift so the calf would hang upside down. A slippery wet mess of just-born hide is not easy to grasp let alone heft, but I managed to lift the calf to my shoulders. Glenn stuck his hands in the calf's mouth and told me he was clearing away mucus. Then he massaged the heavy critter's body. My arms shook as he explained that without the normal pressure of natural birth, we needed to clear the newborn's nostrils and lungs.

He snatched a hanging scale off the wall, and we weighed the nice bull calf. Ninety-two pounds. A big boy, too large for this momma to handle on her own. Pleased to see him breathing, I lowered him to the floor. He tucked his legs beneath his body and blinked at us.

EVERYTHING'S FINE EXCEPT MY PRIDE

But we weren't done yet.

Now we had to get momma back onto her feet before she hip-locked, a type of paralysis that will claim cows after an arduous birth like this one. Bruised around the neck and hind end, she outweighed us by at least nine hundred pounds, and the arrival of her firstborn hadn't exactly been calm or easy. Now, two cowboys, or rather, one weathered old cowboy and a wannabe cowboy, pushed and shoved and lifted until she stood on trembling legs.

Watching this new momma's instincts take over as she cautiously approached her calf, gave him a sniff and a lick, then settled in to clean him, released a mountain of joy in my heart. The rare grin on Glenn's face told me this calf would attach to his mother, and vice versa. Despite his decades, he echoed my wonderment over new life.

Later when I crawled into bed, instead of sleeping I replayed every moment. The life of that calf and his momma, cradled in Glenn's hands. Without him they both would have died. If I hadn't found the right lever, the heifer would have died. My pride at the evening's events descended a notch or two. Next time, I'd be quicker. And before the next time, I'd study that device thoroughly, so I knew which lever did what.

Then my cynical side wondered if Glenn saw not only new life but another $500 with the birth of the calf. I hadn't glimpsed that in his grin, but the man kept surprising me, and I now knew how destitute he and his wife had been before we'd swooped in to buy the ranch and save the day.

I lifted my hands in front of my face, though I couldn't see them in the dark Wyoming night. I'd saved a life with these hands, held brand new life. Far more important than squabbling over a student's dirty, old couch.

10. BIG RIVER, BIG TROUBLE

Not calling me a morning person would be an understatement bigger than the state of Wyoming. But on the ranch, at least during calving season, I endured a never-ending 5:30 a.m. wake-up alarm.

At 5:50 a.m. I'd find Glenn sitting in the cab of the ranch pickup truck. He'd nod but remain silent, and as I stepped into the cab, a straining complaint of oil against metal perfectly mimicked how I felt when I rolled out of the narrow mattress in the frigid trailer. That grumpy old engine didn't want to start any more than I did.

The minuscule electric heater at the foot of my bed barely exhaled a sigh of warmth, though it struggled mightily. Cold, cranky, and creaky, I'd crawl out of bed. It was my own fault. As seemed to be the case most every weekend, Glenn and I talked late into the night until Martha shooed us off to bed. She knew what we'd face today. Full-on calving season, with 125 mommas heaving and straining and sweating to push out new life into that cold, dark night. Or morning. But the stars still twinkled. Guess they didn't know any better.

Like all ranchers, Glenn bred the cows early, so calves would be bigger in early fall when feedlots wanted to buy young beef for grocery store shoppers. But this meant birthing took place in the dead cold of winter, as opposed to when nature intended, in a growing, warm, and greening land.

Zero green for us that morning. Shadows of deep winter looked over our shoulders, and a crunch of white snow complained underfoot. Here and there, thin drifts of ice snuggled up to tufts of long-dead grass. My breath unfurled in the air as I fumbled to close the passenger door. I found that white mist more telling than any thermometer I'd ever studied, and the hot tea in my belly turned cold, despite the heavy boots and Carhartt overalls I wore, along with two sweaters, a jacket, gloves, and a lined, flapped cap. Wyoming winter. Icicles pierced your nostrils with each breath; fingers grew clumsy and thick.

Just the night before Glenn had again lectured me about how a rancher has to constantly check his calves and cows during the height of calving season. That meant twice during the night and again at first light. But not even a hint of blush dared peek out that cold, barren morning. At first it didn't occur to me to ask why he hadn't awakened me for those other two trips. Then I realized he'd let me sleep in on this cruelly cold morning, yet there he was, seventy years old and raring to go, despite heart trouble and even less sleep.

Time for me to get tough and cowboy down. Or was it cowboy up?

As I settled onto the truck's stiff-with-cold bench seat, I remembered talking to a battered old rancher at a rodeo once. Hat pushed to the back of his head, he'd grumbled and groused between spits and spurts of chewing tobacco about contrary momma cows—that they always dropped their calves between the darkest part of night and wee light of morning. With me trapped against a rail fence and unable to back away, that old rancher expounded for an hour or more on his theory that this first-light timing was related to feeding expectant mommas hay and cow cake—a compressed pellet of beet pulp, corn, grain, and vitamins—the day before they birthed. He'd spat one final time for emphasis, then said disgustedly that his neighbors ignored his advice and always ended up with newborns facing life at the coldest and most perilous time of day.

Glenn and I fed all my expectant mommas cow cake just the day before. As we'd spread the cake, he'd expounded again about how liquid protein was okay but more expensive and harder to monitor than feed cake. And he monitored everything. Every lost piece of cake or double-fed momma meant less profit. Glenn's habit of holding his ranch together, literally with baling wire, applied to everything. He made sure the cattle ate right, and he made sure each momma got her share, but no more.

The pickup, a dilapidated old Chevy, nearly stalled as Glenn revved the engine and tried to coax warmth into its reluctant metal parts. Then Glenn warmed up his mouth and started in on the first of his daily lessons.

Big river, big trouble.

I thought he alluded to the river's danger during calving season. Yet I knew that the very same Laramie River he condemned this morning provided life-nurturing water to the ranch, otherwise the hay crop and meadows would shrivel to brown during the intense heat of July and August. High summer in Wyoming is dry and windy. Always windy.

We set out.

Glenn carefully steered the pickup through the minefield of rocks on the under-maintained road used mainly during calving season. At the river's edge he gunned the engine and we broke through a thin layer of ice, tires skidding on rows of carefully laid submerged rocks as we crossed the North Laramie. I looked back over my shoulder, down about a hundred yards from what had become our daily river crossing. Five calves played on the ice floe in a slippery exploration. It looked as if they dared each other to go farther until one small black calf landed—smack!—on his tummy, hooves splayed to the four corners of the compass. The others scattered back to the safe haven of the shoreline.

As we bounced across a particularly large rock, Glenn proclaimed, "Remember to keep your bearings greased. Once," he said, "while Martha and I was shopping in Denver, my right front wheel fell right off this truck, right there in downtown. It just fell off." He'd apparently washed the underbelly of that old truck too many times, crossing the river at that very same place. Sixty calving seasons behind him—this would count as sixty-one—and he hadn't let up yet. This truck had seen fifteen grueling seasons. As for me? I'd stayed up too late. Boohoo.

In the shrub-lined valleys of the hills, the winter calving area, we strained to see through the frosty windows. The trickle of warmth crawling from the defroster wasn't earning bragging rights over the one in my trailer, but we didn't really pay attention. Instead we looked for signs of cows in labor or for newborn calves standing at attention on shaky legs, ready for our brief inspection. Glenn knew each cow's favorite birthing spot. As we rounded a corner, Number 144 stood dead ahead, a newborn calf already sucking momma's teat. In the glare of the headlights, momma glanced sideways at us but didn't stop licking the afterbirth from her calf's still-steaming black hide.

Just the night before, I asked Glenn why we didn't use the smoother-riding and more dignified horses for our early morning review, rather than rattling around in this old pickup truck. That morning I found out why.

Glenn stopped the truck close to cow and calf and said, "I'll tag this calf. You keep an eye on his momma. Ol' Number 144, she's real protective."

With the gentleness of years, Glenn sidled up to the pair and took hold of the slippery calf. I moved away from him, waving my arms to distract momma from Glenn. The calf gave up sucking to look askance at Glenn as momma backed off a few paces to press into a bush. Glenn pierced an ear tag—#6144—onto the calf's right ear while proudly proclaiming to me, "A real nice heifer." As he pulled the scale out from his calf aid kit and tried to lift the calf, Number 144 apparently had had enough of this intrusion into her new daughter's morning feed. Momma lowered her head and charged like a bull charging a matador.

I yelled, "Lookout! She's coming." At least I knew better than to leap in front of her to try and stop a thousand pounds of pissed-off female.

Funny how I levitated into the pickup's flatbed—I would never have guessed I had it in me to leap like that. A single-bound, like Superman. 'Course Glenn, with his years of experience, made it look easy as he hopped sideways like a rodeo clown sidestepping a bull to put the truck between him and momma. We were both glad to have good Chevy steel between us and that angry cow.

Early morning idled on as my mouth watered in anticipation of the massive breakfast Martha undoubtedly had underway. We checked the rest of the regular birthing spots, then headed back to the river crossing. I noticed the black calves that had earlier skated on the river's crust no longer played on the shore. Good. I squinted and rubbed away the frost coating the glass.

Shit.

One had fallen into the river. I could see its head above the water and ice.

Glenn morphed into a race car driver. He ran that old pickup through the river, pulverizing the ice into snow-cone mush. Without pausing to even take the truck out of gear, he jumped out of the cab and into the river. I'm not talking some gentle stream here. This was the North Laramie, and the fully submerged calf bobbed below the waterline as the rapids tugged that besieged new life toward the deadly ice downstream, an ice floe that covered fast water for nearly a quarter of a mile. Unable to touch the river-bed, he wrestled against the deep water. If the calf rolled beneath the ice, it would die. If he stayed in the river much longer, that too would kill him.

Glenn lunged forward like an icebreaker. He grabbed the black, furry mass, raised the water-soaked head above the torrent, and hugged the calf's body to his chest against the Carhartt emblem centered on the bib of his overalls. He pivoted and slipped on the slick rocks that paved the riverbed, struggling to find his footing.

I stepped forward, then back, tap-dancing on the edge of the river like some two-stepping fool. We could both drown, trying to save what amounted to $500 worth of calf. But concern about Glenn, his heart, and the crushing cold made up my mind. I leaped forward. If we both went down, Martha would never find us, not until spring. I had to get Glenn out of that river. Fast.

He staggered, sank into the water to his neck, straightened, and with what looked like his last smidge of energy, threw the calf halfway to me. I grabbed two hooves and heaved the critter out onto the icy bank, then turned back for the waterlogged rancher, pulling him out in turn.

Ice formed on my face and neck as water soaked through my gloves and up my sleeves. I had to get Glenn, and if I could, the calf, back to the ranch house before all of us froze.

Behind me, the truck still idled—I'd thrown it into neutral when Glenn jumped out—and both doors gaped open.

That old rancher outweighed me by at least fifty pounds, and with his soaking wet Carhartts, it was more like one hundred pounds. The calf, not a newborn, probably weighed in at 125. Somehow I half carried the pair of them to the truck and pushed Glenn and the soaking wet critter onto the wide bench seat, though the calf's head lolled down into the foot well. I turned the heater controls to high, and warm air exhaled from the vents as I scraped into first gear and headed back to where we'd started that morning.

Glenn's wife met us at the stoop. How had she known? The sound of the engine revving toward the house must have alerted her. She'd played out this drama before. Martha tugged open the passenger door, leaned in, and said, "Bring that calf into the kitchen." Then she guided her husband out of the pickup and helped him shuck his clothes, nagging all the while about a hot shower. I staggered behind. The spotless, warm kitchen was empty when I stepped into blessed warmth with the calf drooping from my arms.

Gray and lifeless eyes. Blank as the ice. Glenn's gallant rescue had been in vain. I lowered the carcass to the floor and slid it across the linoleum, back toward the door to put it outside. Martha reappeared, brandishing a pair of hair dryers, reminding me of some famous sheriff from the Old West flourishing a pair of six-shooters while confronting an outlaw. She clicked the plugs into the wall, and dual whining crazed the night as ice turned to water atop the matted fur of the lifeless critter on the floor. I stared. Couldn't she see the death on her kitchen floor?

Ten minutes must have passed as that calf's coat curled and dried, puffing up into a handsome, shiny black coat that would make any member of 4H proud. Shucking my wet coat, I turned away for a moment to spread it across a kitchen chair to dry. When I turned back, I know I gasped. One eye of that calf rolled back from gray death, and his nostrils expanded and contracted—shallow but persistent.

The other eye rolled down, and the calf trembled and kicked to right itself, even though it could barely hold up its head to look at the strange surroundings. Table legs. Chair legs. My legs and Martha's. The whine of the hair dryers stirred up Glenn's two ranch dogs. While they'd mostly ignored this frozen adventure, both whined and paced, ears folded flat against their skulls. Too much hot air, too much wet, and too much noise for them. Before breakfast, no less!

The calf heaved itself up to stand on four soft little hooves. Clearly ready to escape this confusion, he swayed. I grabbed him, and the two of us wrestled for dominance, but I held him in place so Martha could continue her salon efforts. A dry, warm, and bright-eyed beast trembled in my arms.

Glenn, who had soaked his frozen body in a twenty-minute steamy shower, trotted down the hall in a new set of dry Carhartts. He paused in the doorway to survey the three of us, and I could see the smile in his eyes. The calf lived. It didn't even belong to him, but that rancher cared so much that it hit me low in the belly. A sucker punch.

If he'd owned that calf, come late summer or early fall, he'd have sold that pretty black critter to be butchered into steaks and hamburger. But the look on his face, in his eyes, told it all. He cared more about that newborn life than his own. He'd no doubt risked his heart to overexertion so many times that this morning wasn't anything special, not to him. But this new life, that was everything. Everything.

Glenn poured himself a cup of hot Folgers coffee as he waited for me to don a dry jacket and gloves. Then we drove the calf back to his bellowing momma, who fussed and fumed and came close to knocking me over as we hauled her baby out of the truck. With a bawling cry the calf bounded off to greet momma's suspicious sniffs, and soon her strange new child didn't seem so strange when he found the breakfast bar and sucked down a sweet drink of fresh milk.

I never saw that calf or its momma near the river the rest of that winter season.

11. HORSE TRADIN'

The whole family came up, along with Tucker and Tucker's girlfriend, Rachel.

Rachel? Tucker's new girlfriend?

Once upon a time . . .

Bossy. Demanding. Arrogant.

When first attending architectural graduate school, I might have applied any or all of those pejoratives to Rachel, then a teaching assistant in the master's program at the University of Colorado. Worse yet, her nickname—"Little Hitler"—remained a sealed-lips secret among my fellow students.

She might have been a talented architect, but her attitude distracted me and others. Virtually nonexistent in the design profession, women had to be strong, tough, and talented to excel in our demanding profession. I'm fairly certain we didn't appreciate that.

Post-graduation, as my professional life flourished, I heard she, with a partner, founded a small architectural design firm. Not too long after, I heard through that very same design grapevine that her firm failed. Did I feel smug? While I've rarely wished someone ill, I think smug might be a good description. After all, the Boulder firm I joined boasted two founding partners, Art Everett and Alan Zeigel, who led the cutting-edge design of significant regional projects.

My own arrogance dimmed when the same 1980s recession that claimed Rachel's firm upended our office too. Strangely those layoffs, reduced hours, and lack of design projects provided me with the opportunity to buy out one of the partners.

Never afraid of a challenge, I embraced that risk along with a handful of new partners. Our skill sets blended well, complementing one another without much redundancy. A few years later, talent, perseverance, and with the steady hand of a great CFO, we grew the firm into a multi-studio powerhouse—one of the largest architectural firms in Colorado.

For those that don't quite grasp the unusual blend of design abilities and business acumen needed to maintain and grow an architectural firm, Ayn Rand's novel *The Fountainhead* chronicles it well. The struggles of a stubborn young architect, Howard Roark, who fights for innovation and refuses to compromise his design and management principles, partially defined and possibly fueled my quest for a new and different reality.

Yearning for close connections to nature, the human spirit, and nurturing rather than ignoring what inspired my passions, set my cowboy boots firmly on the fork in the road leading to ranch country. At least on the weekends.

Turned out, after giving up on private practice, Rachel went to work for the City of Denver. Her personality, smarts, take-no-prisoners attitude, and tough outlook rocketed her to the position of Planning Director. She and Tucker crossed swords regularly, between her profession and his as a high-level consultant in real estate investment and development. The respect they felt for one another shifted to friendship, then romance.

Talk about two ducks out of water. If not for me, I know Tucker would never have considered exposing his Kenneth Cole loafers to cow manure. And Rachel? She couldn't possibly be interested in ranching.

She wasn't.

But she *was* interested in shedding her professional burdens with true friends. Ones that didn't suck up to her because of her close working relationship with Denver's mayor and powers that be. Friends who would always have her back. Plus, she'd lasered in on the blue-ribbon fishing we boasted on the North Fork of the Laramie River.

Fishing?

Of course, not worms and bobbers and lures type fishing. No. She pursued our elusive silver fighters, Donaldson trout, with dry flies by the name of "Elk Hair Caddis" or "Dave's Hopper."

Over the years, I had learned, sometimes the hard way, that first impressions might not be accurate. Such was the case with Rachel. She fell in love with the ranch.

The peace and simple physical work we shared helped all of us negate the stresses of our careers. Unlike the rest of us, Rachel also had the pressure of coping with a shitload of politics and press, with the entire City of Denver populace poised and ready to chew her ass.

Though I don't believe I ever voiced it, I often wondered if the trout she snared represented her professional adversaries. Her position within the Denver bureaucracy required not only architecture but skills in personnel management, nonstop political savvy, an understanding of development, and plain old guts to help shape the resurgence of a historic but dilapidated downtown.

One of the first things out of Rachel's mouth that day had something to do with the hushed stillness of the land—that she could hear herself breathe. I felt that way myself every time I headed north. No matter that our list of projects grew exponentially, my heart always downshifted when I drove past the battered old mailbox.

We relished our walkabout. The constant Wyoming wind had apparently taken its cue from us, seeking a hiatus from everyday responsibilities. Truly a miracle in and of itself. We walked to the north end of the property to look at the rock formations. They reminded me of the Flatirons outside of Boulder. Then we toured the southern hayfield, where my emotions soured. We'd lost the water rights to that field. Pissed me off royally. Turned out that if you didn't keep water flowing to a field, over time, you lost the rights to that water. It seems our cobbled-together rock dam had washed out in the spring flood of 1962—decades before we'd ever set foot on the ranch—and as it was never rebuilt, we had no way to gravity-flow water to the pasture. Water is king in the semiarid West, with water value outstripping land value in some locations.

I think I only pretended to have gotten over my pissed-ness a week later when we met Glenn to head out to the feedlot. Water meant life on any ranch, and even though I needed to bury my frustration, I knew myself well enough to recognize I'd chew on that lost pasture for some time to come.

The feedlot, a dusty slab of land crisscrossed by steel-rail fences in a maze of quarter-acre pens worthy of the confusing images in the lithograph *Relativity*, held primarily black angus, though a few brown-and-white Hereford cows stared out at us. Narrow rows of concrete feed troughs lined each pen, and six- to seven-foot-tall mounds of manure claimed the center of each. Various buildings housed a store and offices and storage barns and silos.

Glenn had decided to keep about forty head of his own, and by the time he sold his steers, each would weigh around 1,200 pounds. A swift and silent calculation of our potential revenue and expense made me grimace as Katie penned a check for our $8,000 feed bill. I reminded myself we were rebuilding, and that took capital. Then there were the tax write-offs we could take advantage of. Even so, I'd crunched enough numbers to recognize how many more big checks we'd be writing, and to me, the completion of a successful architectural project with ecstatic clients also included a bottom-line profit.

Competitive? Me? I craved success as much as I'd yearned to be a cowboy. More than once, when describing our efforts at the ranch to friends in Boulder, I joked about the sucking sound wafting my way from up north. Think of a sound akin to a calf at a momma's teat, sucking on our checking account. That's what I could hear. But we were in this for the long haul. And we *would* succeed.

On our way back to the truck, Glenn waved a man over to introduce us. Bill Windmeier. We chatted about him building us a new horse barn, with either five or six bays, and the design for our new corrals. My hand hovered protectively over my wallet, but both needed to be done.

Back at the ranch we met with Jake Garret, whom we'd hired as our new ranch hand a couple of weeks before. A wannabee bull rider who wanted to cowboy—but not too hard—Jake previously spent his summer months drywalling massive ski chalets in Vail. I soon learned he wasn't the smartest tack in the barn, but he knew enough, generally, to handle his ranch assignments. I knew enough to keep an eye on his efforts.

We first met Jake and his wife Hallie at a for-sale ranch on Sybille Creek, south of Wheatland, where they acted as caretakers. After Glenn told us the pair would be looking for work when that ranch sold, we hired them.

Jake had been out riding the colt he bought, whom he'd named Rusty. He and Glenn spent a couple of minutes figuring out when they would drive down to Boulder to pick up our horse, Black Jack.

I'd learned some lessons about horses and cows since we bought Black Jack, and I suspected neither Jake nor Glenn would be particularly impressed with our first foray into horseflesh, and they certainly were not.

Years ago, one spectacular blue-sky Fourth of July, leading the small-town parade down the main street of Frisco, Colorado, trotted the most magnificent paint horse I had ever seen. Ears up and eyes wide, decorated with Native war paint—a red circle painted around a white eye—and carrying a rider dressed in a full warbonnet headdress, the horse appeared to understand the importance of his position as the head of the parade. After the parade I simply *had* to ask if the horse was for sale. No surprise though; the owners exclaimed that they weren't interested in selling him.

My love of horses infiltrates my first memories of visiting my grandfather's farm near Denver.

Each August, no matter where my father's job with Chevrolet Motor Division had taken us, we would travel to Colorado for three weeks, and as a five-year-old, I couldn't wait to get back to the farm.

During my youth we'd called many places home. I labeled myself a "General Motors brat," akin to an army brat. Detroit, Pittsburgh, Portland, Danville, and Cleveland stand out, but the weather, especially the humidity, and the congested eastern culture didn't interest me. Nor did California, with its crowded "fruits and nuts" populace. I yearned for crisp cool mornings, sweeping vistas, and the friendly, open culture enjoyed by my Colorado home state.

During one of our visits my grandfather saddled a small black-and-white pony that my brother and I rode around the farm. In college I often found myself astride a "rent-a-rig" horse when visiting a national park. Led by a sometimes bored, or more frequently nervous, cowboy, depending upon the experience level of those they guided, those dusty, plodding horses spent their days walking nose-to-tail. Should one of their normally placid beasts actually dump some unsuspecting tourist whose boast of years of riding proved false, those cowboys knew a bevy of lawyers would descend faster than locusts. I enjoyed those rides for their scenery, not the riding experience.

Though not the best name for a novice rider, the first horse I bought, Buck, came from a middle-aged cowboy working at a cutting horse training barn near my home in Boulder. My empty barn in the backyard needed a horse! Many years later I realized how that cowboy sized me up, as horse traders so often do. I had no regrets though, as Buck, an eleven-year-old buckskin, had such an even temperament, one I'd even describe as a unique kindness, one that I've never seen or heard of in a horse since. Always quick to turn and easy to stop, I found Buck perfect for my backyard corral "push button" riding experience.

In my naivete I didn't even hire a veterinarian to check Buck before completing the purchase, instead trusting in a cowboy's handshake. Decades later, with numerous horse purchases and sales behind me, I knew that every horse has at least one or two issues, whether physical or mental. Books are filled with chapters of potential problems, describing colic, cribbing, bowed tendons, swayback, and so many other ailments that they can often be more confusing than helpful.

With Buck, I soon learned that one of the most important phone numbers to memorize is that of your veterinarian. That's how we got to know Doctor Mark, a well-traveled, honest young animal doctor who, upon his first visit to our barn to perform a basic checkup of our newly acquired and "perfect" horse, asked, "Did you know this horse is blind?"

Shocked, and if truth be told, devastated, I shook my head in denial, exclaiming, "Absolutely not. How could he be ridden so beautifully and so well?"

Patient beyond his years, Doctor Mark went on to explain that our beloved new horse had a disease caused by cows and that Buck was totally blind in one eye and partially blind in the other. I think that young vet could tell that I already considered Buck a member of the family, so Mark explained the pros and cons of owning a blind horse, ending his statement with the warning that Buck would eventually become totally blind.

Inside an arena or corral, a blind horse can function well, taking cues from its rider. Out in the wild green yonder? A totally different story.

Reluctantly I called the previous owner. He immediately offered to take back the horse, no doubt wincing at the damage that might ensue to his sale barn if a well-respected veterinarian began passing the word that the local horse traders sold a blind horse to an unsuspecting family. It was a sad day when Buck stepped out of our lives and back into the cowboy's trailer. Little did I know that this would be the best horse I'd ever own.

The cowboy persuaded me to follow the trailer back to the sale barn to see what other horses they might have in lieu of a straight cash refund. Since we still wanted a horse, I acquiesced, and for an additional thousand dollars, an elegant five-year-old named Black Jack joined our family. While smooth to ride in an arena, Black Jack had a wild glint in his eyes. Though not long in the horse business, even I realized that horse's name provided a glimpse into its personality. I acknowledged that wild edge, but swayed by his beauty, the architect in me admired the gelding's glistening, muscular body and almost perfect conformation; aesthetics matter to design professionals. We are trained to truly *see* what we're looking at.

Not about to be taken advantage of again, when the cowboy backed him out of the horse trailer and released him in our pasture, I found myself gazing upon the Mister Hyde side of Black Jack. High-strung prancing, head tossing, rushing the fence, that gorgeous horse now intimidated me to the point that I asked the cowboy about the change in behavior. Though I nodded in agreement when the man replied that Black Jack simply had to get used to his new surroundings, I also said I'd drop off the thousand dollars *after* the vet check.

I felt nothing but relief when Doctor Mark visited our barn the second time. He said Black Jack was in excellent condition, that he in fact knew the horse and that he was a reining horse. That explained the odd, smooth shoes Black Jack wore on his rear hooves. Trained to do circular show patterns followed by a long slide to a stop, butt low to the ground, those wide flat shoes helped horses to slide, sometimes for as long as twenty feet before grinding to a halt.

I ground my own teeth when Doctor Mark replied quietly to my question about the change in temperament. It seemed that one trick often used by the horse traders at sale barns was to ride their horses extra hard before a potential buyer dropped by. Tuckered out and sometimes lightly tranquilized, a high-spirited horse presented itself as calm and easy to ride.

As competitive then as I am today, I decided to master Black Jack. As my riding skills improved, he turned out to be a good horse in the arena, though still flighty around the farrier and trail rides. Quite the looker, his shiny jet-black coat never escaped a cowboy's glance.

With my horse buying prowess logged at zero for two, about six months later I headed to the paint sale pre-auction at the Denver Stock Show. There, horses warm up in front of potential bidders, so buyers can see the horses in motion rather than posing on the auction block. A big nice-gaited paint caught my eye, and as he took several laps around the arena, the beat of my heart increased. The English tack worn by the paint distracted me. His saddle should have been a heavily tooled western rig, trimmed in silver, with the edge of a red-and-black Navajo blanket just visible. Could it be? Frisco? The Independence Day parade? Yes! As the handlers exited the arena to lead the paint back to his rented paddock, I cut them off at the pass before they could even unbuckle that dinky saddle. How could I ignore destiny? I bought JC before the auction, private treaty.

When we owned the ranch we owned many horses, each with its own personality and quirks. Buddy, Tuff, Tiny, Oreo, Cyclone, Duke, and Murphy come to mind—working horses for a working cattle ranch, used to the rocky Wyoming landscape. Arena pets didn't thrive. With miles of sparse tundra unnavigable by trucks or four-wheelers, and ornery half-wild black angus to move and separate and doctor, an efficient rider, a true cowboy, bonded with their cutting horse. A thing of beauty, a cowboy and his best horse became virtually telepathic and could definitely anticipate every move an evasive steer might make to avoid capture.

I shook myself out of my reverie when Glenn stretched his legs long and started talking bull. As in, we needed to look at young bulls soon; they'd cost about $1,200 each. And we needed to see about ordering fertilizer for our hay fields. That would cost about $0.60 an acre if we rented the machinery to spread it ourselves or $3.00 an acre if they spread it for us. We also needed to buy seed—an 80/20 mix of grass and alfalfa seed would grow into a perfect hay pasture.

Glenn then suggested we sell the old cows—those that shouldn't be bred again—right before the Fourth of July. It seemed that the demand for hamburger would often be higher over the holidays, and prices would go up.

12. MONEY MONEY

No April showers for us. Instead snow and a cold wind waved hello as we crossed the Wyoming/Colorado border. The strong gusts made it easy to decide to stay in town instead of trying to sleep in the tin can, plus we'd already made plans to look at eighty acres south of Wheatland, a parcel of land that we could buy for haying. While the initial expense made us balk, we'd already figured out it would save money in the long run by nearly replacing the annual hay purchases needed to supplement our pasture-raised hay.

I couldn't help but shake my head the next day when we heard about the Two Bar, a nearby ranch established in 1871, listed for $4 million. Try amortizing that against beef at fifty cents a pound!

Later in the month I tallied all of these events when our 1932 JD Tractor and the Ford both quit. Just plain quit—like in the old television show *Green Acres*, that antiquated tractor blew one last smoke ring out of its stack. My wallet, and that of our LLC, came close to deflating faster than we could fill them.

A few weeks later my whole family came up for the weekend, and we arranged to meet Bill White and his wife. Mostly for fun, we decided to drive to the Two Bar Ranch. Curiosity had twisted our tails, and we wanted to compare that ranch to ours to see if we'd spent too much or got a good deal. A historic spread with a classic ranch house, cottonwood trees flourished along Sybille Creek, marking one boundary of the Two Bar's well-groomed hay fields.

After that weekend, we decided we needed to get into the habit of carrying the checkbook with us. We headed to an auction after visiting both properties, where we bought a John Deere four-section harrow and looked at tractors. Big and small. Prices ranged from $17,000 to $25,500.

Ouch. Then we looked at a smaller used 2640 tractor with an asking price of $15,000. Better. But should we buy new or used equipment?

Next up, the Norell Ranch's horse sale, where we looked seriously at five horses and ended up buying three—an eleven-year-old sorrel and two four-year-old sorrels, all from Texas. Spent almost $11,000 on the trio, but we weren't done yet. Needed tack for all, and oh yeah, that matter of a new barn to house them! Ka-ching!

Bill Windmeier had rough plans ready so we could review construction details and his estimate. I thought it more than ironic that the $12,000 to $13,000 equipment barn would cost about what we'd spent on those three sorrels and their tack. I recognized that construction in Wyoming and the ease (or lack) of permitting kept costs lower than in the Denver metro area and also accelerated the schedule, reducing the overall cost. A lesson learned, one I wished I could apply to our firm's architectural projects heading in the opposite direction, as far as complexity and bureaucracy.

I spent that evening summarizing what we'd spent to date and projecting what revenue our steers would bring in over the next two years. Then we drafted our "need," "want," and "wish" lists before cracking open a bottle of wine.

Payday at the architectural office, and I couldn't help but again mention to my partners at oz Architecture that the hungry money pit in Wyoming needed constant feeding. Replacing the infrastructure, building up the herd, and buying luxuries like horses cost far more than we'd budgeted, and I still didn't grasp how full-time ranchers could do it—how they earned a decent living, season after season, decade after decade. They didn't.

I'd had my own fill of lean times, exemplified by the 1980s recession triggered by the oil shale bust. Despite twenty years of success, our architectural firm, founded in 1964, operated hand-to-mouth. Projects were scarce and each week found the partners scrutinizing every expense, no matter how small. Sadly, they laid off a few staff members and reduced hours for everyone else.

I soon learned that living on 60 percent of what I'd previously banked didn't work. With a car literally held together by duct tape and wire, I finally abandoned my pride and asked my father about the possibility of moving home. Temporarily, mind you. I was shocked when he said, "Absolutely not!"

A self-made, successful executive who put himself through college after serving his country at age twenty during World War II, my father, along with my mother, had survived their own lean times. It made them stand tall. From them I learned the definition of hard work by starting my own lawn mowing business at the age of fourteen.

My father always urged me to *think* about my work, to study what created success or failure. That advice led to an ethic infused with the goal of working smarter than others. If I did work smart *and* put in more hours than the architect down the street, I assumed new projects would come my way. During a recession, such is not the case.

The lesson I learned during those lean years modified my approach to the goal every architect has: to design a much-admired and celebrated project. Instead I came away with the philosophy that even the most utilitarian or unglamorous building should and could be designed to exceed that owner's expectations and goals.

I respected ranchers like Glenn who always lived on a thin financial edge. Fluctuating calf prices, struggles with worn-out machinery too expensive to replace, and coping with Ma Nature's regular tricks, chewed up a rancher's energy while often spitting out pennies on the dollar.

At least I didn't have to worry about whether bank loans would be called before the next calf sale or if beef prices would once again be manipulated by powers I couldn't influence, let alone control.

Another two weeks, another weekend. We arrived in Wheatland on Friday night and again decided to stay in the motel, with its nice running water, solid (though not soundproof) walls, and clean towels. On

Saturday morning we hauled the boys out of bed before dawn, much to their regret, and drove out to the ranch at 6:00 a.m. to gather in cows and calves from the Camp Creek pasture. I rode Glenn's mare and our new ranch hand, Jake, rode Tricksy. He'd ridden Buddy, one of the new sorrels, the day before and thought the gelding neck-reined well and didn't appear to have any bad habits other than laying his ears back when you fed him. I'd seen that habit before, and it didn't worry me as long as Buddy didn't decide to take a bite out of one of us or his corral mates.

Today Glenn's mare and Tricksy did most of the work. Ears up, they concentrated on their job, turning and stopping and leaping into a run, anticipating the steers' every move before I could react. Glenn drove the truck and hauled cake.

Ignoring the occasional whiff of truck exhaust, we enjoyed a picturesque morning, enriched by swaths of yellow flowers, purple locoweed with its hairy leaves, and mounds of dusty green sage. Antelope turned tail and fled as we persuaded bawling, belligerent cows to assent to our way of thinking. Go *that* direction, not *this* one! Persistence is good, and good horses are even better.

Glenn and Jake taught us how to run the calves through the chute. We learned how to administer two vaccines with a gun-like injection device. Glenn branded our four new bulls faster than I could wipe the sweat from my forehead.

Branding—a skill I wanted to become adept at. That, and roping. Of course, I wanted to be the best at both, though I knew folks raised on a ranch would have an ease with ranching skills that I would envy and always strive for. Being a weekend cowboy, it was difficult to master the techniques learned from birth by boys and girls raised on a ranch.

With the bulls' bellows echoing in the background, we huddled around the list of cattle, our inventory, so to speak. Number 20 hadn't joined in today's fun. Glenn rolled his eyes and mentioned a couple of hiding places she favored. Another lesson learned. Half-wild range cattle had long memories. We'd have to track her down.

13. THE MEETING

Tucker, the boys, the dogs, Katie, and I all headed north to Wheatland. We stopped at Brown's on the way up to buy a hay swather from Larry for $6,000 plus trade-in of Glenn's old swather. My partners then proceeded to tell me our "new" used swather looked like crap. Sure, the seat cushion needed to be replaced, but other than that it looked fine to me. If it runs well, that'll tell the tale.

Then the shit just piled on.

The trigger? Glenn moved two of the horses, JC and Oreo, out of the pasture near the house.

You wouldn't think moving a couple of horses could spark a stampede of acrimony, but before we could hear the clip-clop of approaching hooves, Glenn's simple suggestion ignited a firestorm. Owner versus previous owner.

Katie and I then had what I think of as "The Meeting."

After she chewed *me* up (and inside out), I understood her point of view. She felt Glenn didn't treat her with respect—that he *always* sought affirmation from me for every decision. Never her. Ever.

I was smart enough not to say that respect is earned or that, despite the decrepitude of the ranch when Glenn sold it, I had a helluva lot of respect for that tough old cowboy. Katie didn't, and he knew it. He reciprocated in kind. We recognized the chauvinistic side of this as well and agreed that Glenn wouldn't change.

"Awkward" could have been my middle name over the next few weeks, and I *hated* that it fell to me to kick Glenn off the ranch. His ranch. His home. For longer than I'd lived.

On July 2 I had a long teleconference with Glenn.

I candidly, and I hope respectfully, explained to him that Katie wanted to be more involved in the day-to-day operations of the ranch, and our current management style of him always seeking my opinion, and vice versa, didn't work. Besides, I *wanted* to side with my wife. Plus I didn't personally own a majority of the ranch—my wife's family did.

A few days later Glenn informed us that he and Martha would move to Wheatland in the fall but that he would remain available on a consulting basis.

As things settled down and as is my habit, I found satisfaction in working more hours, then even more, at both the office and at the ranch. I put the cable on the rail of the new deck on the old fishing cabin and installed ceiling fans. My architectural career blossomed when I landed a new design project, headquarters for a manufacturing facility that nicely filled in the gaps in our staff's schedule. And when Katie finally deigned to return to the ranch, that first night, as we sipped wine under a full moon, the dance of the fireflies flitting through the moist air down by the river elevated our mood.

The bumps in the road smoothed. Sadly our untroubled journey didn't last.

Though I'd managed to extinguish the Katie versus Glenn conflagration, all too soon we learned about a large fire north of the ranch, started by some idiot from Colorado trying to burn anthills with gasoline.

A month after that, a major storm hit. Three inches of water sloshed in the rain gauge, which wouldn't have been a problem by itself. It was the four inches of hail accompanied by flooding that wrung us out. With the lake full, the river running out of its banks, and Johnson Ditch breaking and flooding the lower pasture, scattering tons of rock and debris, I hoped we'd seen the end of our "everything comes in threes" difficulties.

But no.

Beaten down by the hail, our large pasture now resembled a rocky, dirty tarmac. So much for cutting our own hay for winter feed. The good news? We did find handfuls of Native artifacts, washed free by Ma Nature's heavy hand, so we started a collection of arrowheads.

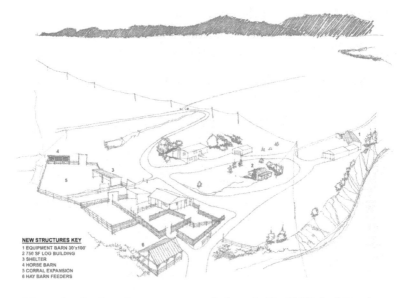

NEW STRUCTURES KEY
1 EQUIPMENT BARN 30'x100'
2 750 SF LOG BUILDING
3 SHELTER
4 HORSE BARN
5 CORRAL EXPANSION
6 HAY BARN FEEDERS

5. Master plan sketch noting new structures built on the Devil's Washtub Ranch. Courtesy Bob West.

Architects. We never stop analyzing our physical surroundings, and the architect in me *demanded* I create a master plan for the ranch. The cowboy in me agreed. Our ranch partners—Katie's family and Tucker—as developers, engineers, or commercial real estate experts, also agreed.

We had a mess of buildings and roadways constructed as needed over the previous century. Now with a built-in architect, we could analyze the big picture and build our way out of that hodgepodge mess.

My close friendship with Tucker, a nationally-respected commercial real estate analyst and broker, began when he, Katie, and I developed a historic loft project in LODO—lower downtown Denver. The dilapidated and creaky John Deere Plow Company Building, built in 1871, and Moore Hardware Building, erected in 1877, faced one another across Fifteenth Street. Both were so frail they could easily have been condemned. Yet with Katie's father's structural engineering firm stabilizing the buildings, my design efforts, Katie's management, and Tucker's real estate savvy, our successful renovation and adaptive reuse created not only fourteen exceptional lofts in a district in the early stages of stirring with "new life" but forged a solid and effective multi-disciplined team.

I delighted in sharing the news with our team, now ranch owners, that in Wyoming, ranches exceeding eighty acres in size didn't have to submit to the county for approvals. No planning board, building permits, or neighborhood meetings! The landowner did need to employ a licensed general contractor to complete the job, but we'd planned on that anyway.

What a pleasure, designing without bickering neighbors and officious bureaucrats looking over our shoulders to challenge or second-guess every decision! We did, however, shock Glenn Harrison more than once.

A drinking deck for the old fishing cabin? How could such a frivolous and money-wasting effort be one of our priorities?

A summer cabin with no exterior decks or patios, built on the side of a ponderosa pine-studded bluff overlooking the river, the view of Laramie Peak snatched my breath. Why *wouldn't* we spend time and money to not only take pleasure in that view but to nurture the fellowship of family and friends? About a mile from the ranch headquarters home, privacy wasn't an issue, so I forged ahead, designing a heavy timber deck that cantilevered out over the canyon wall to open the view in either direction, up and down the river.

After construction, and with our cabin lights extinguished, the dark sky greeted us as we stepped out into the night. Shooting stars and satellites swept across the heavens, with the waterfall cascade of Milky Way stars providing a potent reminder of what lay beyond. Often nursing more than one beer and a few aching muscles from our ranch work, we relished the solitude. Raw nature: the rush of water below, wind, and the occasional sound of night critters soothed our ears while the unpolluted dry western atmosphere provided a clear lens to the skies. Reminding me of my youth, fireflies created their own dance of constellations as they glided above the willows at the edge of the river.

6. Upper cabin alongside the North Laramie River. Courtesy Bob West.

7. Sketch of drinking deck addition to upper cabin alongside the North Laramie River. Courtesy Bob West.

8. Completed drinking deck addition to upper cabin alongside the North Laramie River. Courtesy Bob West.

Next on the list, we built a five-bay metal storage barn with a heated shop. Our investment in new equipment needed protection from the scorching summer sun and thick Wyoming blizzards.

After spending those brutally cold winter nights in the tin can of an RV trailer we'd used that first winter, I pressed for a new cabin, sited on an old foundation between what we called headquarters (the existing house currently occupied by Glenn and Martha), near the cattle and horse barn. I wanted to be close to the action, especially when our hands took days off.

A relatively inexpensive prefabricated log home kit with two bedrooms and one bath fit the bill. With a traditional look, it could be erected quickly, and we could handle most of the interior finishes. The warm spirit of coming home rolled over me as the walls climbed up from the foundation.

Next up? A larger horse barn including an owner's tack room, separate from the ranch hands' tack room. Tack and saddles are expensive, and each horse had its own bit and bridle, so we wanted to protect and organize everything necessary for our growing horse stable.

In about 1920 Glenn and his father built the most remote river cabin on our property when the Harrison family purchased their first parcel of Wyoming land. In their move from Johnstown, Colorado, the Harrisons sought a more prosperous life, though I learned from Glenn that they soon questioned whether a single cow could survive on the short grass in such an arid clime. Locals assured them that cattle were as tough as the buffalo that'd once thrived on the blue grama, western needlegrass, fescue, and brome. In fact they claimed the dry prairie foliage provided more protein than lush river grasses.

Although we'd saved the century-old LODO buildings, that river cabin hosted a myriad of problems. I chewed and chewed over whether to renovate it, let gravity take its course, or speed the demolition process with a front loader.

Glenn and Martha laughed and shook their heads when describing life in that quaint but feeble structure. On the worst of winter nights, the low ceilings, partial foundation, and little or no insulation found Martha stoking the wood stove and leaving the oven door open so they wouldn't freeze. Then there were the pack rats who now claimed the cabin as their own. If we swept the floor, a week later the big-eared rodents had collected new treasure to decorate their abode: small stones, sticks, mounds of grass, pine needles, cactus leaves and spines, delicate bones—any and all of Ma Nature's debris. Inevitably our local skunk contingent also preferred those rotting walls.

Snugged in close to the river, though not where the cabin itself would flood, shaded by ponderosa pines, the site couldn't have been any sweeter, except we had to cross the river. Winter access? Roadway flooded in the spring? Yes to both. Both could be solved.

I stopped chewing.

We decided to build a new log cabin with two bedrooms, a bunk room, a large great room, and a full kitchen. Though still on the wrong side of the river, the cabin would be big enough for us to host a dozen or more guests. Large decks wrapped around the perimeter, strewn with rocking chairs and porch swings, would give us a place to congregate even in bad weather, as I planned a wide roof overhang.

Our industrious and creative contractor solved the river-crossing issue by buying two old flatbed trailers. With the wheels and suspension elements stripped from the flatbed itself, concrete abutments on each side of the river supported the thick, now side-by-side, steel panels. Topped with treated three-by-twelve-inch timbers—instant backcountry bridge! No guard rails, of course, as this was the wild, wild West!

Our last *major* project included a three-stall horse barn and roping arena near the cabin.

Whew!

Dead tired of politicking projects through approvals, and my daily, sometimes hourly, and frequent nighttime commitment to managing at least my share if not the overall architectural firm, I decided—needed—to take a sabbatical. Four weeks wouldn't create too many hiccups for my projects or partners, and I desperately wanted to refresh and recharge my creative spirit *and* spend time with my wife and boys.

So for twenty-eight sublime summer days we fished, rode horses and four-wheelers, practiced roping, taught our underage boys to drive my old truck, hiked, ate, watched falling stars, and rarely sat still. Never good at sitting on the deck to gaze at my navel, we explored long-abandoned homestead ruins dating back to the 1800s. One not too far from our new cabin still stood. A square stone tower, about twenty feet tall and maybe ten feet wide, with a charred wood ceiling, blackened interior, and clanking steel hoists, had served as a smokehouse for a century or more. The hand-laid stones remained pleasing to the eye, and more than once, I found myself circling the sturdy construction, envisioning slabs of beef, deer, or other game animals being hoisted into the heights of the chimney-like structure. A small fire of dry pinion branches to create smoke as much as heat, with the entry door closed, only tendrils of blue would have reached through the cracks.

Surprisingly, perched above the ceiling of the tower was part of a cistern to store water hand-pumped from below. That original Harrison cabin had running water, supplied by gravity and ingenuity!

I tore off the broken-down and rusted cistern and added a pyramidal shade roof and aspen log ladder. The best lookout tower or fort ever made. Beware of the Super Soaker water guns our boys snuck up the ladder!

Forty-five days later I drove up on a Friday night with my stepson. Relishing the temperate fall weather, we kept the windows down in the truck most of the way, though Wyoming's ever-present wind did have its way with my cowboy hat when we stepped out of the truck.

After unloading the insulation I'd purchased for the shop, we drove up to the lake to see whether the water level had dropped. Then we walked up the canyon to see what flood damage remained. Even now, clear

9. Sketch of vision for the stone smokehouse. Courtesy Bob West.

10. Stone smokehouse repurposed as a play tower/fort. Courtesy Bob West.

pools of water and drifts of fallen vegetation decorated the landscape. The fishing was good, though. We caught several rainbow trout, probably fifteen-inchers, and one smaller brown, maybe eleven inches long.

The fishy smiles fell off our faces when we returned to the cabin and spied an uninvited guest waiting for us: a ten-button rattlesnake sunning himself next to the front door. At least I saw it; my son didn't. He trotted toward the front door and a pair of lunges followed him. First mine, as I grabbed his shirt collar and lifted him up and away from the lunging and fanged aggressor. I don't think my heart could have beat any faster as I backed away, Little Walter in my arms.

While I dislike trophy hunting, rattlesnakes fall in a different category, especially with kids and dogs around. I lifted my stepson into the bed of the truck, grabbed the spade at his feet, and before our unwanted guest could sidle away, lopped off that snake's head. As Little Walter often hunted with his father, I waved him over as I pulled out my pocket knife. He hopped out of the truck and stood beside me, watching with rapt interest as the snake's body writhed for a few moments before it realized it was dead. After I skinned the long body and rinsed away the blood from my hands and the handsome, brown, diamond-patterned skin, Little Walter helped me tack the skin to the wall so it would dry in the sun.

I met Glenn the next morning and he gave me a water right abandonment form for his water rights under the lake. When he handed me a bill from John Rhodes for his part-time work, I thought I caught a quick flash of amusement. Couldn't be certain of that, not with his ever-present poker face.

Jake picked up the hay roller from Chugwater, and the three of us spent some time looking it over.

14. AN HONEST-TO-GOD ROUNDUP!

Mid-October of '96 found us driving north late one Tuesday, arriving in Wheatland at around 10:30 p.m. Despite the late hour, rather than heading straight to the ranch, we took a detour, motoring through the "drive-thru lane" for margaritas at the local liquor store. Open liquor containers in the car? Not a problem in Wyoming, as long as you weren't drunk. In spite of the lovely beverages, once at the cabin, we hurried our typical routine of getting settled in for the night since we were meeting Jake at 5:45 a.m.

The clamor of the alarm clock pushed us out of bed. With a few hot beverages in our bellies and bowls of cereal for the boys, we high-stepped it out to the horse barn.

An honest-to-God roundup! On horseback! Yeehaw!

I rode Buddy, Katie rode Duke, and Jake rode the new, unnamed horse. We rounded up the cows and calves, checked our counts, and sorted out ten heifers to keep and breed. When the big truck arrived we loaded eighty-four calves for the Torrington sale.

The excitement of controlling so many half-wild beasts, the thud of hooves, an occasional curse when a calf bolted free, twisting in the saddle as I tried to watch every which direction at once—I'd envisioned this for at least a decade. I'd smelled the dust and chaos and sweat. I'd eaten that grit in my dreams.

The chorus that rose above it all, though, the lamentations of the mommas calling for their babies, I hadn't ever imagined. A raw sorrow reaching for the heights, sung by that black angus choir, echoing ever upward in a cadence heard over the years—the decades—the centuries. Their chorale shivered in the air, raised dust, and prodded the hair on the back of my neck without cease for three days. We heard it when we

11. Sorting cattle in the Devil's Washtub Ranch corral expansion. Courtesy Bob West.

drove off and when we returned. We heard it in our sleep, at the sale, from the surrounding ranches, and in our dreams.

At the sale, the cacophony of sound and scents escalated long before we met up with Glenn, Jake, and Jake's family. Already rattled by the emotions of the morning, I made sure to stay between Glenn and Katie but soon realized I didn't need to. Katie had won the war, and Glenn ignored her, preferring, or possibly pretending, to focus on the sale. When we first arrived, the auctioneer's gavel regularly pounded "SOLD" at about sixty-three cents a pound.

I soaked it all in. The intensity of the sellers, stoic folks, for the most part, jumped from person to person, family to family. Before long, I caught hold of the rhythm and grasped it by the tail.

A few more pennies per pound? Maybe that old tractor could finally be replaced. A few less cents? Gonna be a lean Christmas. And I do mean trimmed to the bone.

I hadn't met most of these ranchers, but many of them were of Glenn's generation. Their lives and livelihood had been dictated by floods and fire and famine. By the price of hay and protein and taxes. By markets they couldn't control any more than they could lasso Ma Nature and bend her to their will.

At about 7:30 p.m. our lot of yearlings were put to the gavel. We bettered the average price by about three cents! High fives and smiles all around, but I couldn't silence the calculator whirring and clicking in the back of my mind. By the time we paid for market charges, yardage, beef council expenses, health inspection, brand inspection, insurance, and trucking, we would net just over $23,000. For the year. Not even a spit in the bucket.

Yet another confirmation of what I already knew. While we would strive for a profit, I'd feel victorious if break-even joined us for supper, say, five years from now.

The bad news kept on coming.

Just before Thanksgiving Jake called to tell me he found glass in the cake. He cleaned it out of the big storage bins as best he could. Glass. Broken glass that would chew up any critter from the inside out if they ingested it.

I wanted to shout, "But wait there's more!" when he muttered that we had a couple of other problems to discuss.

He'd arranged for the vet to stop by to make sure the cows were all pregnant and ready to be vaccinated. All good. As an afterthought he'd also asked the vet to age the cows. It seemed the question of age had been on Jake's mind for a while, and Glenn became tight-lipped and surly when Jake complained that the majority of our mommas were old gummers—called that because of ground-down teeth from years of grazing—and that we could probably only breed them another time or two, if at all.

For dessert Jake said that Glenn had been driving off the main road, which ruined any chance that the flattened grass would grow during our hot summers. As a deterrent, Jake suggested he spread some big rocks along the sides of the road in those areas.

Dazed, disheartened, disappointed, and disillusioned, I couldn't decide which emotion gripped my heart, shaking respect for Glenn out onto the floor. I think I told Jake to go ahead and spread the big rocks.

We'd already told Jake to go ahead and sell more cows over the next couple of weeks, but now we'd have to rethink that. Would we be better off keeping our own young heifers to build up the herd, or should we buy two-year-olds? We had to have breeding stock.

The icing on the nonexistent cake? Beef prices had been on the rise. If we'd held on to that first batch of calves, we would have made an additional 10 percent or so, less the cost of the extra feed. Talk about a poker game. Buy. Sell. Hold 'em. At least I didn't feel as if the local "greenhorns" were the only ones who'd sold before prices went up. Many an old-timer did the same that day.

Our next trip north, we decided once again to stay in town. Before heading out to the ranch, Katie and I drove by another forty-acre parcel of land listed for $60,000. We stopped, walked along the edge of the property, and kicked a few clods of dirt as if that would tell us the quality of the soil and how well it retained moisture. Then we drove over to look at a small ranch on the market for $82,500. Comparing the cost of the land to buying feed made no sense, but my gut told me we should get out the checkbook. So many properties had already been carved into thirty-five-acre "ranchettes" that produced little or nothing in the way of crops or beef, that acquiring this small one made sense. We could put the land to work while values continued to rise and possibly subdivide sometime in the future. I didn't want to contemplate that happening to our big ranch, though.

The next weekend we didn't head to the ranch until Sunday when we planned to meet Tucker and Rachel. After our arrival and chatting with Jake, we helped feed the cows, then walked up to the lake, where flood damage still surrounded us.

Focused on picking our way through the debris, about a half mile from the water we veered east. I don't know who shouted first when we stopped, but I think we might have been shaking our heads in unison, left to right, left to right, as we stared at the large pine in front of us.

Shredded by the force of the flood, broken fingers of low branches pointed our way. The tree probably topped thirty feet, but it wasn't the magnitude of the tree damage that caught our attention. What startled us had been wedged in between the thick, needle-laden branches at about eye level. Angled downward out of the tree, our lost canoe might have been used as a condor's nest if one of those massive birds ever traveled to Wyoming and enjoyed such narrow confines for her eggs.

Tucker surprised us all with a terrific New Year's present. He bought a new, and very serious, telescope. Now we could spy on the hawks nesting on the butte across the river, and if Tucker wanted to stargaze, he could set the telescope to pivot in tandem with the rotation of the earth. We decided to leave the telescope in the living room or on the outside deck instead of moving it in and out of the bedroom Tucker and Rachel typically used.

Dinner at Vimbo's, Wheatland's local joint, morphed into a year-end discussion of our efforts. With the plates cleared and fresh beer poured, I thumbed through my journal, reading snippets aloud. We laughed and laughed. And yes, more than one moan punctuated our joy, but in the end, when I raised a toast, I honored family and good friends, goals underway or accomplished, and new goals set.

While we weren't yet cowboys, we'd learned a helluva lot, so the greenhorn appellation no longer served. It made me proud.

I nursed my beer, fell silent, and closed my journal.

All four of us held high-stress jobs with more than ample responsibilities.

oz Architecture's rising growth curve meant proportionally more guidance and increased staffing, which created a snowball effect. More employees meant more projects which often led to larger projects and the need for more employees. Demands on our professional services also escalated. Everything from an increased desire for green design to revised building codes to lawyers surfing owners' associations for litigation opportunities to more computer-based design and 3D presentations pressured us into a constant evaluation and revisions of our goals.

Katie managed a handful of large real estate projects and also shouldered primary responsibility for our boys' various events. Tucker's commercial real estate expertise and consulting services had become even more sought after, and Rachel, as head of the City of Denver's Planning Department, well, she had the entire City of Denver to plan.

I raised my beer in one final end-of-year toast, expressing my appreciation for the ranch, for our ability to go back to the land, and not only for the mental challenges of learning how to cowboy down but for the physical efforts as well, which offered a swift and necessary pop-off valve for stress.

15. THE TROUT WHISPERERS

March of '97 at the ranch found my alarm clock raising Cain at half past five. The cowboy way: rising at dawn. Not my cup of tea. Most mornings, though, after *two* cups of steaming green tea and a few slices of bacon, I would gladly step into Duke's saddle to ride through the herd, checking them over for signs of distress, pending birth, or new injuries. If nothing unusual caught my attention, I would feed the cows and bulls.

One particular day Jake left for Casper, so after the morning cattle rounds, I picked rocks until my back ached, wondering if we should start building low rock walls as we'd seen in Europe. It seemed as if the soil, through freeze and thaw seasons, birthed new rocks every time I turned around. Rubbing my sore muscles, I headed over to the cabin to wait for the arrival of our local trout whisperers, Jennifer and Joanne. Nine-to ten-inch-long Donaldson trout—a sterile cross between a rainbow and steelhead—cost $2.65 apiece plus delivery. After today, next year's summer angling fun would increase exponentially.

As the pair of Js acclimated 270 trout to the forty-three-degree temperature of our river next to the lower cabin, we had a long discussion about the potential increase to the value of the ranch if we improved the river itself by creating a true fish habitat. I think it was Jennifer who mentioned that some of the nearby ranches stocked fish for executive retreats and charged $500 per rod per weekend. For that we needed deeper pools in the riverbed and would have to get health certifications for the fish. Health certifications? For fish? Yep. And we'd need an experienced backhoe operator—one who understood fish, deep currents, and how to "walk" their heavy equipment down the river without stirring up silt or trouble. I nodded and absorbed their fishy lessons. Regardless of whether we decided to pursue such upgrades, watching those Donaldsons slip-slide into the water made me want to grab my rod and reel. Fly fishing right out the back door!

During my midday cattle rounds, I noticed Number 53 moaning. Last week her calf fell into the river and drowned, and even though she now shared a calf with another momma, her loss remained undiminished. Don't tell me animals don't have feelings.

Tucker came in Saturday night, and on Sunday we slept in really late, until about 7:30 a.m. After our slim breakfast—toast and tea—not your typical cowboy fare, I showed him how to drive the tractor, and we fed the cows. He motored along as I rode Duke. As we circled behind a low hill, we found Number 132. She'd prolapsed. Her uterus, which looked like a mottled, supersized eggplant, swayed from her hind end.

Tucker fetched Jake while I kept an eye on stoic 132 and her trembling calf.

I heard Jake approach in the ranch truck, and he must have skidded to a hurried stop, as a skiff of dust drifted over the hill before he and Tucker trotted around to join me.

Muttering to soothe the critters, Jake sidled past momma into the calf's blind spot and wrapped an arm beneath his chest. In front of momma, he frog-marched the still-damp critter forward to lure her into following them to the barn. She lowered her head and glowered at them but didn't take one step. I couldn't blame her. If my insides had been pulled outside, where they didn't belong, I wouldn't want to walk anywhere, either.

I heard Jake sigh as he tugged the calf over to us to hold as he trotted back around the hill. Coiled rope in hand, he returned and roped the cow with one easy-looking toss.

As the loop tightened around her neck, she bolted, by God!

Remember those cartoons when a character is dragged hither and yon for what seems like forever, with an occasional cactus sliding beneath their butt? That's what happened to Jake. I flinched on his behalf as 132 skipped through a mound of prickly pear cactus and over a tumble of football-sized rocks. With her purple balloon of a uterus bouncing along like a deflated bustle, she dragged Jake all over the field and then down into the river, where she sat down in the water, body language announcing quite clearly that she wouldn't be moving again.

I thought that momma was pissed, but she couldn't hold a candle to Jake.

He didn't say a word as he stomped back to the truck, but the look on his face would have turned ice water into cheese.

I jumped up on Duke, ready to save the day by galloping to the main ranch house to call the vet, and that damn horse dumped me in six seconds, flat. Launched over Duke's head, I nearly kissed the ground in front of him, landing hard on my hands and knees. He snorted as he looked down at me as if to say, "What you doing down there?"

My wrists hurt like hell.

After Jake cooled off, he and Tucker maneuvered the truck over to the end of the rope that had trailed behind 132 while I nursed my wrists, along with my pride.

They tied off the rope to the trailer hitch, and Tucker pulled Number 132 out of the river with the truck. Now even more pissed off, 132 looked like one of those rodeo bulls released from the gate and consumed by bucking and head-twisting, but they quickly dragged her close to a tree and tied her head off so she wouldn't hurt herself.

Impressing me as one brave critter—or maybe as hungry—the calf tottered to her side.

Jake said he'd head back and call the vet. With Tucker holding Duke's reins, I wondered whether to ask if the vet could also look at my wrists.

When big momma Number 82 wandered over to check on all the commotion, she ran at Zip, my littlest dog. He yipped once before cowering beneath the truck.

What a circus! Me, cradling my wrists, my scaredy-cat dog, and poor ol' 132. I prayed Jake hadn't torn her inside-out parts open when he dragged her out of the river.

Finally, the vet showed up. He tied Number 132 even tighter (think rope so tight it could be plucked like a guitar string), washed her clean, shoved that uterus back inside, administered antibiotic shots, and sewed her shut.

I swear that vet had almost choked her to death by the time he stowed his sewing kit.

I changed my mind about mentioning my wrists.

Realizing I couldn't easily step into the saddle, I waved Tucker up onto Duke and told him I'd ride back to Jake and Hallie's cabin in the truck. I think, though I can't swear to it, that Jake covered his mouth to keep from laughing when I tried to open the truck door. By stacking one thumb on top of the other, I managed to push the button on the door handle, and I held my hand and forearm rigid as I hooked the handle with my fingers to open the door.

Jake did stop snickering long enough to tell me he thought maybe a too-tight belly strap on Duke's saddle might explain the bucking bronco antics.

Now he tells me.

After dinner, proud that I'd handled the silverware without overt difficulty, I muttered my goodbyes and clomped out to my truck to drive back to Boulder. I managed the door handle without histrionics. Smug, I tried to turn the key in the ignition and couldn't. Literally. I didn't know whether to laugh or cuss, so I sat there for a while.

16. THE SALE BARN

A year had passed since we sold that first batch of calves bred under Glenn's watchful gaze, one full cycle of a cattle operation. Winter feeding, calving season, branding, summer grazing, haying, and now, today, the culmination of all our efforts: the sale of calves whose inception, birth, and life, *we'd* overseen. I'd pulled some of those babies. I'd watched them cavort and eat and grow on our ranch. Just as we'd grown.

Today we'd be compensated for our work—for the risks we'd taken physically *and* financially. Thankfully we weren't doing this for the money.

The morning started loud with our unrepentant alarm clock jolting us awake. After a night of too much drinking and talking late into the starlit evening, the mechanical squawk sounded even more brazen than it had in the days before.

We'd pushed the mommas and calves down from their summer pastures, where the calves romped and skipped about for weeks, learning to eat grass but still pausing to enjoy a regular and reassuring suckle on momma's teat—warm milkshake days when a calf often sported a white mustache. Having survived coyotes, winter and summer storms, lightning, and ice on the river, only to make it to this day, when man would break their natural bliss to fulfill his quest for money and, eventually, a good steak.

No horseback riding for us today. Everyone would be on foot.

Today would be stressful for the calves as we separated them from their mommas, and we hoped to minimize their anxiety as much as possible. Stress caused calves to lose weight and made them more susceptible to disease. At the sale, buyers would look at not only breeding but age, history, stature, strength, and of course, weight. With a paycheck based on that weight, we wanted quality to provide the leavening.

As gray light faded to gold, we walked with Glenn around to the back of the scattered herd. Already rattling the bucket of cake she carried, Martha stepped into the corral and stopped next to the gate. Cows raised their heads and ambled her way. She kept rattling. Most of our old mommas recognized that sound and knew it meant "come and get it."

We spread out on the far edge of the herd and, with raised arms and an occasional slap against our own thighs, urged our black angus toward the corral.

Cows going through a gate remind me of sand sifting into the bottom of an hourglass. The sand bunches up at the top, and only a few grains can slip through the narrows. If the sand gets stuck, everything stops flowing. Same with our herd. They bunched up and groaned and tried to break away, but we kept them pointed into the funnel.

Glenn trotted ahead to slip into the corral.

All hell broke loose.

Think allemande left, but half the square dancers instead choose to do-si-do.

Those old cows figured out Glenn's moves lickety-split. They did NOT want to be separated from their babies and were NOT going through that gate.

A veteran handler like Glenn, whose every movement had a purpose and every stare down shifted a cow, made separating a 1,200-pound momma from her 350-pound eight-month-old calf look easy. I'd heard the saying "cows have more time than cowboys, so cows always win," but I hadn't taken it to heart until I tried to mimic Glenn's actions and failed. Calves streamed past me, escaping back to their now frantic mommas.

Spitting dust and maybe a few curses, and with Glenn leading the way, we square-danced around those critters 'til the last calf squalled all the way down the main chute of metal fencing, where Jake and Hallie waited to separate the heifers from the steers.

Meanwhile the scraping rattle of a boxcar-sized empty aluminum trailer presaged the arrival of a large tractor-trailer made specifically for today's chore. Numerous air vents cut through the tall siding, and two levels of internal ramps and dividers created a double-decker transport for calves. Expertly handled by its capable baseball-cap-wearing driver, who wasted no effort maneuvering the cumbersome rig backward into the sloped cattle chute, we hurriedly selected thirty "replacement" heifers, the lucky ones.

Those lucky ones would stay on the ranch and next year become the new mommas of another generation. An endless loop. Old cows, after ten or so years of loyal service, and without many of their teeth left, grew thin and could no longer carry a large healthy calf or process grass to produce milk. They were the not-so-lucky ones and would soon be sent down the hamburger road.

We opened the gate between the steer pen and sloped ramp to coax the now trembling creatures into the truck. Pushing and bellowing, rolling their eyes, the calves tried to evade our guiding hands, the ramp, the cold steel railing. They feared for their lives, and rightfully so.

Apparently impatient, or possibly thinking it would be less traumatic for the calves if they'd accept the inevitable, the driver jumped down out of the cab with a shock stick in hand.

I flinched.

The humane treatment that Glenn advocated and taught ended now. It didn't matter that my boys and I had named some of the calves, that they would sidle close to eat cake from our hands. No.

The business end of the cattle prod facilitated the loading as none other. After all, the driver had a schedule to keep and many ranches to visit. Our precious calves were neither unique nor special to him.

I spat dirt from my mouth.

Certain the last eight or ten would never fit in the trailer, I felt some pleasure in the difficulties the driver would now face, but the calves all fit. The driver slapped the gate closed, and after handing him a single piece of pink paper, a signed branding certificate, off he went. Down the dusty trail.

The heavily laden trailer didn't make nearly as much noise traveling away from the corral.

A scramble of hides and heads and legs followed the truck as mooing mommas trotted alongside the fence-lined road until the trailer faded from sight.

Our lucky thirty, still confined in the corral, called to their mommas, and I could swear they sounded less frantic, like they knew they'd been spared. While we would soon move them to a distant pasture to begin a weaning process from their mother's milk to grass and cake, today their mommas sidled close to the fence and thrust their heads between the railing to lick and comfort their young ones.

Glenn waved us to the trucks, but I stood next to the fence for a few minutes.

He'd already told us that first-time mommas not attuned to the cycle would wait at the end of the corral for hours—sometimes days—waiting for their calf's return.

The mosh pit of bellowing and shuffling trampled my enthusiasm for the day. I sighed and turned away.

The drive to Torrington and the sale barn started with a stop at the local café, The Wheatland Inn, our community social hub. Virtually every morning of the week, a train of pickup trucks dusted themselves off, traveling from dirt roads to gravel to pavement, and parked in that hospitable lot adjacent to the Inn. Chevy pickups mingled with Fords and Dodges, dings and dents and scrapes and even mottled patches of rust, telling tales of hard use and years of service, though all sported those wonderful Wyoming plates with their bucking bronco and cowboy symbol—a sign that the heritage of cowboy country lived on.

It seemed like the entire town occupied booths and round tables in the café. Everyone knew Glenn and greeted him, so it took at least eight or nine minutes for us to wend our way through the tables of leather-faced cowboys and farmers. I shook hand after hand and immediately became

THE SALE BARN

aware of my silky-smooth city-slicker grasp against rough palms, with more than one rancher missing fingers or thumbs, no doubt casualties of roping mishaps or lack of concentration while working with heavy machinery. I wanted to tuck my thumbs into my palms as I designed buildings with my hands; the prospect of losing a thumb disturbed me more than I cared to admit.

We finally settled at a table, and as was nearly always the case, everyone but me ordered coffee, black, from an older waitress with many years of experience in her craft. She handled the orders with the skill of a dancer for half the café, never wasting a movement, able to carry armloads of breakfast plates with heaps of scrambled eggs and bacon, or chicken fried steak on potatoes, to her eager and hungry audience. When I asked for green tea, she smiled sympathetically and said, "Honey, you must be new. I got Lipton." Of course.

As I overheard conversations from adjacent tables, I soon realized that this was where great political debates started and, at meal's end, were tabled for another day. The local gossip included the weather, the price of corn, and what calves were selling for.

During that meal I realized how Glenn's "behind his back" nickname of "Teardrop" came about, as he capped each conversation with a negative note. If it had rained, it was too muddy; if it hadn't rained, the fields turned into concrete. Present, future, or past, he didn't discriminate; every condition created "Oh, woe is me" results.

With the imminent arrival of a hungry lunch crowd, we abandoned the café and regularly scheduled political debates for our drive to Torrington. That hour or so of rolling hills of grass prairie and rock buttes soothed my pissed-ness, and when we blew past Fort Laramie and the small, in-between town of Lingle, I again looked forward to the auction.

In Torrington, a town of about five thousand people, the well-used sale barn loomed large, a peeling, painted, white wooden structure built specifically for cattle auctions. In the parking lot, an occasional white pickup truck braved the sea of blue half tons, many pulling stock trailers. As we parked I could see an eighteen-wheeler had backed up to the stock pens at the rear of the property. Bawling calves trotted down the ramp of the double-decker aluminum cage into the stock pens while three newly arrived eighteen-wheelers waited patiently for their turn to unload their unhappy loads. Black angus dominated.

I'd already decided we should pick up some white-faced calves, usually crossbred from Herefords. Once too often I'd skidded to a stop at midnight with my heart in my teeth to avoid a black steer chewing his cud while lounging smack in the middle of our ranch road. A white face would at least give us a fighting chance at spotting a black critter after full dark.

We headed for the wooden walkway above the pens to peer down on what seemed like hundreds and hundreds of calves huddling together and mooing in unison as they tried in vain to hide from the strange noises surrounding their temporary quarters. Feeding racks mounded full of hay and narrow troughs of fresh water calmed some, though most shoved and searched in vain for a familiar moo. We searched, too, in a hurry to find our cows, wondering whether we'd already missed their stage debut. Finally Glenn waved us over to a pen with all black cows wearing our familiar brand: quarter-circle C slash.

Only a few pens contained all-black steers and heifers, with the majority sporting a blend of black, white-faced black, brown, and even a few all-white. During his seventy years as a Wyoming cowman, Glenn, ahead of his time, believed that black angus produced a better beef cow, and that's all he raised or championed.

The cadence of the auctioneer drew us into the sale barn as surely as dogs follow the scent of hamburgers thrown onto the grill. A temporary bout of blindness greeted us as we stepped into the darkened structure, what with a handful of spotlights pointed center stage and our backs turned to the bright afternoon sun.

Blinking away tears, I counted at least twenty rows of worn wooden bleacher seats encircling the room, all focused downward at the manure-covered, ground-level stage that wasn't really a stage. It functioned as a stage, and the three auctioneers—all well-dressed and wearing matching black cowboy hats—treated it like a stage, but in fact, that layer of old manure covered an oversized scale, one large enough to hold forty calves and their handlers.

An electric signboard stood next to the auctioneers. Once the next lot had tromped onto the stage, whether one heifer or forty, the signboard displayed the lot number and total weight of the stock up for bid.

Then the auctioneer's singsong cadence began, first with a description of the lot, its heritage and age, and any other bona fides such as inoculations.

Buyers studied the carefully orchestrated parade of beef, young calves, steers for feedlots, and heifers to build a new herd or diversify bloodlines. A few weeks back, the sale barn had published thin booklets with descriptions of the stock to be sold, so the ranchers had already read about the lots offered up today.

The crowded bleachers held young and old, families and singles, all clad in cotton shirts and jeans and boots and hats, with more than one ranch dog sitting patiently at their owner's feet. I could tell by the anxiety that traversed the barn when an owner's stock came up for sale. Frowns. Smiles. Sorrow. Every emotion I could imagine.

"Can I have $200, 200, 210, 220 ... Then can I have $230 ... 230 ... 230."

The price increased while most of us sat quietly. Or so I thought. Instead of raised hands or nods of the head, nearly imperceptible signals indicated a buyer's interest. A slight tip of the hat brim, a touch of one finger to the nose, a lifted chin—how the spotters positioned in the crowd managed to spy these subtle signals impressed me. I quickly learned to remain frozen in place during the frenzy of a bidding battle.

Pen after pen of cows entered the ring, each auction lasting about sixty seconds. A few lasted longer when superior quality captured everyone's attention or when two buyers became locked in battle. With our stock scheduled for 3:30 in the afternoon, during a lull, I murmured my concern to Glenn that all the buyers would be gone. Glenn assured me that folks knew him and his quality calves. He said buyers would wait for our lot. Sure enough, when the first of our calves—sorted into five groups based on size and sex—stepped out onto center stage, my chest puffed out like a proud new papa.

Our shiny black calves looked fantastic. That day, clear-eyed, feisty, and well-fed calves abounded and bounded around, but ours trotted faster and lifted their hooves higher. Right?

The auctioneer cleared his throat, took a sip of water, then began his song. "Now lookie lookie here, black cows from the Glenn Harrison ranch in Wheatland. They don't come any better than this, folks." And the bidding began. Our calves, or Glenn's reputation for quality beef, or most likely both garnered attention, with a lot of thirty-three steers averaging 550 pounds on the block for about three and a half minutes. A long battle, perhaps even the longest of the day.

I'd seen a number of ranchers leave the barn after their cows sold and could often tell if they were pleased, but not always. For many this was simply another day in this difficult business, and they had no control over the final value of their stock. Ranchers might be able to grow or shrink their herds based on current values, but most didn't have that luxury. They needed the cash.

We watched a few more lots sell after ours, though none as high, so we enjoyed a few congratulations and handshakes as we walked to the office to collect our check.

While pleased with the money, as this represented the sole sum of revenue for the year, I couldn't help but shake my head. How in the *hell* could a rancher live off such a meager once-a-year check? The bottom trough of a ten-year cattle cycle held us, with its low, low prices for calves, but that simple rectangle of paper reinforced—yet again—Glenn's decision to sell the ranch. He and Martha wouldn't have lasted another year.

Pondering that on the way back to Wheatland, my good mood faded as I again became morose over the lively critters we'd sold. I hoped they would be treated humanely.

17. SCOURS, SCOURS, SCOURS

Scour my soul?

Scour the herd?

Scour our goals?

All of the above.

The early months of 1997 found me agitated. Again. Somewhat dependent on the time of year and whether I ranched alone, or almost worse yet, with one or more of my inexperienced partners, my nerves escalated, despite countless lessons with Glenn, my improved skills, and vastly improved knowledge.

Virtually all of the "real" cowboys I hung around with during my Wyoming jaunts had lived and breathed the cowboy way since birth. I hadn't even sat on a working horse until age twenty-eight. Riding a paint pony at my grandfather's farm near Golden hadn't readied me for this life. Yet at age forty-two I kept trying to cram unfamiliar skills into my somewhat mulish limbs. Not exactly mulish. My body mostly proved as willing as my mind, but neither had lifelong instincts for the depth and breadth of cowboy chores. I had to think through lists of tasks, whereas a born-and-bred cowboy would simply spur his horse, grit his teeth, and spontaneously get the job done.

Calving season intimidated the hell out of me. Starting in February and for the next few months, I prayed that my ranch hand wouldn't ask for any time off or fall ill.

What if I had to pull a calf? I could and did assist, but Jake could do the job without me. The reverse? I didn't want to find out.

What if a momma prolapsed? Would I be able to shove her uterus back in?

What if a momma carried twins, and during birth, the pair tangled up inside of her like those twisted metal puzzles that could only be untangled in a certain order? Untwining two unborn calves by touch, guiding the first of eight legs into the world in the proper order, required inordinate strength and infinite patience, though you had to work quickly so fatigue wouldn't claim the momma. Too slow, and all three would lose their grip on life.

What if that happened during a blizzard, in the middle of the night, near the river, and a pack of coyotes lurked yards away, noses raised in the frigid black night to inhale the scent of steaming blood and offal, seasoned by my own sweat-laden fear? What would I do then? I'd planned on ranching to be fun and fulfilling. Not a nightmare.

Not to mention my dread of that certain time of spring presaged by brisk rains. Anticipation of those rains made me shy as a brand-new colt. A fuzz of sweet green grass would creep across the winter-brown prairie. Snowmelt would fill the river, carving deep, dark holes for the trout to lurk in during the heat of summer, and all of the calves would have made their appearance. The last blizzard would have sighed resignedly before slipping up to the high country for a summer snooze.

What made me so leery of the loveliest of spring days?

Scours.

Just as I disliked visiting Mexico because of the cramping claims it made on my digestive system, despite my careful attention to diet and drink, scours could wreak havoc on a young calf. Untreated, dehydration would cause discomfort, but then pneumonia would wade in, followed closely by death.

Scours. Even the word soiled my mouth.

My angst had less to do with doctoring the disease and more to do with cornering the calves so I could play doctor. The Marlboro Man made roping look easy. Spur your mount, stand in your stirrups, and gracefully swing that lariat loop above your dusty black cowboy hat. A swift flip of the wrist and the loop flew effortlessly over the calf's head, swallowing horns and head in one gulp to snug around the throat of a bawling, bucking, chest-high, mostly wild beast whose sharp hooves could break a man's thigh bone.

Me? The Marlboro Man?

Nope. Not even the Marlboro Boy.

On one particular April weekend, my dread turned into reality. Jake had taken a few days off. Katie and her brother Brian, his girlfriend, and my sons joined me up at the ranch. Two full-grown men, two full-grown women, and two get-in-your-way boys. Not to mention 160 units grazing on tasty spring sprouts of grass. Perfect.

Cold rain pounded the ranch for three days, but today, as we saddled the horses, clear, high skies graced Wyoming. With that luminous mid-morning blue towering overhead—a blue that deepened to the darkest of sapphire in the evenings—we had little to complain about. Sun chewed on our wrists where skin peeked out between gloves and shirt sleeves, but our wide-brimmed cowboy hats shaded our eyes and faces.

We headed out, catching up on gossip while laughing at the boys' antics. A mile or so from the cabin, we startled to a heart-pounding stop when we flushed a pheasant. He sailed smooth and low over the cacti and tufts of tall grass. A less flamboyantly dressed harem of ladies probably lurked nearby, but we couldn't spot their soft brown plumage or bright peeking eyes.

We waited and watched, caught our breath, then rode on, cresting a low-rising hill where we stopped to look down on our herd. Our herd. That had a nice sound, and I repeated it to myself as I urged my brown-and-white horse forward. He twitched his ears and stepped confidently down the hill, unafraid of the black beasts spread in a loose, wide arc in front of us. As we drew close, the calves shied away, trotting behind their momma or a nearby aunt or cousin to hide.

I reined my horse to a stop, my stomach sickeningly tight with too much green tea.

Shit.

Worse yet, scours.

A couple of the calves raised their drooping heads to gaze at us. Eyes dull, legs stiff and awkward, a telltale streak of brown striping their bony rumps, they wobbled as they stepped behind their mommas to hide. Tails limp and motionless, the poor calves already looked dehydrated.

Oblivious, my riding partners, family and friends all, chattered on behind me. I took a deep breath. Time to cowboy up. Jake wouldn't be home for two days. Our calves needed immediate doctoring, and I would be their vet.

I twisted half around in my saddle to look pointedly at Katie and Brian while gesturing at the herd. I'm certain my voice sounded as desiccated as a dry riverbed as I choked out the problem we faced. I asked them to stay away from the herd so it wouldn't spook—but to stay close enough to keep an eye on them—while I raced back to the barn to fetch the blue pills and what I privately thought of as one of a repertoire of torture devices we now owned.

Picture a massive sword swallower twisting and writhing beneath your knees as you try to wrench open his mouth, stretch his head back to straighten his throat, then imagine shoving eighteen inches of a gleaming chrome plunger holding a two-inch long cylindrical blue pill down his throat. Pray you don't take a detour into his lungs along the way, press the handle, and phase one is done.

Phase two? Before you release the bawling, thrashing, pissed-off sword swallower, you have to tug a stick of crayon-marker out of your pocket and clearly mark his head so you don't mistakenly catch him again the next day and give him an overdose of those potent, blue pills. Now you can jump away, hoping the patient won't kick you in the head as he scrambles to his feet. No matter how sick, calves have exceptional aim.

The magic blue pills, like Tums, do work wonders. And you did just save that critter's life. A little kiss—er, kick—in return is only fair. Right? My stomach sloshed as I turned my horse.

When I returned, the rodeo was on! Brian, who carried all the requisite cowboy gear with him at all times when on the ranch, said, "I'll rope 'em." He squinted at one of the weaker calves, nodded at him, kneed his horse toward the shivering creature, and thundered down the hill. Every single cow and calf, all of whom had been standing and staring, bolted. In every stinking direction. Undeterred and in hot pursuit of his targeted black calf, Brian urged more speed from his mount. Brian raised the loop in his rope, swung it carefully, and released!

Missed.

Brian reined to a stop and carefully recoiled his rope—we'd both learned you could easily twist off your thumb if you handled it carelessly.

I flinched as Brian again spurred his horse toward the same trembling calf that'd stopped to catch his breath. The calf bawled once, pivoted, and scrambled away. Gracefully Brian swung the three-foot-wide loop above his own head, knocking his cowboy hat loose. Down it fluttered, only to be skewered by a huge yucca. His horse, more experienced than any of us, flattened his ears and stretched his neck to stay out of the way of the rope. Brian ignored both and flung his loop in a beautiful arc.

It landed beside the calf.

Brian skidded to a stop, coiled his rope, threw, and missed again.

And again.

And again.

And again.

And yet again.

Blowing hard and ignoring his lost hat, he turned his horse to trot back to us.

We revised our strategy.

Katie, Brian's girlfriend, and the boys would spread out and calmly herd the cows toward Brian and me. Then Brian and I would bookend a calf, which would (hopefully) allow Brian a close enough range to rope the recalcitrant patient.

How many miles we trotted that morning, I couldn't guess. But two hours later we stopped. We'd herded sick calves all over the prairie, with pissed off mommas running interference, and we'd burned up at least three days' worth of calories. My boys sucked it up and stuck it out, but they'd hit a wall. With no new ideas, Brian and Katie said it was time to head back to the cabin and call the vet. I didn't remind them that we'd still have to rope the calves for the vet.

I decided to stay. Some of our calves might die if we didn't treat them, and with only one of us near the herd, I thought they might settle down. I could try a calm new approach.

First I looked all around, as I wanted to make sure no spies lurked about, not even my family. Here I sat in the middle of a 3,200-acre ranch that ran four miles long and two and a half miles wide, and I wanted to make sure no one could see me.

I walked my horse closer to a couple of the sick calves, dismounted, and carefully laid out Brian's rope in a ten-foot-wide loop, hiding it with tufts of grass. Think Wile E. Coyote and the Road Runner. That smart bird never fell for the trap, and I didn't think my calves would either. By then I could have sworn they'd all taken some secret evasion course . . . or watched cartoons on Saturday morning.

Finally, though, after eight or ten tries, I snared one by the rear leg. Maybe that particular calf had slept in late one Saturday and missed the key episode the others viewed.

Now, though, I wished I had company. I'd poked many a pill down my dogs' throats, and I'd doctored calves the previous spring, but then, Jake or Brian or Tucker had been draped, full-body, across the beast, pinning it to the ground. Now it was me, myself, and I. And the sick calf.

I couldn't sense any weakness in the thrashing legs and muscle that I'd snared. That calf pulled hard, and for a moment, the rope sizzled through my gloves, echoed by a flush of heat that burned my palms. I stepped over the rope, wrapping it around my backside to gain some control, then I slowly pulled the rope with my right hand while holding the slack with my left and discovered yet another reason to wear

Wranglers. That stiff cloth sheathing my butt not only cushioned the rope but also kept it from sliding easily.

The calf morphed into an espresso-swilling kangaroo, jumping and hopping and plunging. In the cartoons he would have been snorting steam.

I took a step closer. The calf skipped sideways. Another step. The calf danced a jig. I pulled in more slack. An arm's length away, I body tackled him. A quick slam to the dirt and I had him. Panting, his tongue lolled out of his mouth, a typical sign of a calf under stress. I suspect my tongue might have been protruding as well.

Careful to keep my balance, I leaned back to pull the loaded steel cylinder out of my belt.

With my knees pressing down on his forelimbs and chest, I stretched that calf's neck straight and held his head steady.

Open sesame.

The calf chewed on the cold chrome cylinder and rolled his eyes. I pressed the plunger and sent that blue pill where it belonged. I pulled the torture device free, and with shaking fingers, groped for the crayon marker in my pocket, drew an X on the calf's forehead, took a deep breath, and leaped backward. Managed not to trip on the prickly cactus behind me.

That calf glared at me, surged to his feet, and wobbly-kneed-it straight to momma.

I squinted at both, looked across my prairie at the crescent of cattle spread out over several acres, and slumped down to sit next to the cactus. I know I lifted my hat to wipe my forehead on my sleeve as I pondered.

It would take me two or three days to snare and treat all of those calves. They weren't rabbits blindly following the same well-worn trail. And I couldn't go to the neighbor and ask for help. Well, I could. But cowboys didn't ask neighbors for that kind of help, not for regular doctoring. So . . . I decided to take a dangerous course. I would wait another day. In twenty-four hours the calves would be weaker. I should then be able to walk up to a sick calf, body tackle him, and pill him. Certainly not the preferred method or the best schedule, but for a cowboy without roping skills, I lacked alternatives. I ached deep in my gut, risking those calves like that. I disgusted myself. For not being skilled at roping. And for being too proud to ask the cowboys on the adjacent ranch to lend a hand. Katie would ask. So would Brian. Not me.

But my risky plan worked. Somehow we lost no calves that season.

18. THE BOYS FROM BOULDER

Architects schedule their workflow by multiple months, as design and construction of a building might take anywhere from twelve to twenty-four months or more, depending on the size and complexity of the project. I'd learned that ranchers planned short-term tasks by the season and long-term by multiple years.

How long would it take to breed white-face Herefords into our entire black angus herd so we could see them in the dark Wyoming nights? A bonus: hybrid vigor would make them heavier at weaning time.

If drought claimed the prairie, would it recover in one season of normal rain or take three?

How many years to amortize the cost of a new barn?

Then there were long-held traditions that had to be respected.

Branding at the Devil's Washtub Ranch had *always* been scheduled for the first full weekend of May. As it was, as it shall always be. In fact each neighboring ranch scheduled specific, historic dates to avoid overlap, allowing neighbors to lend a hand across the region. Even though we abided by that traditional schedule, this year, things would be different. We'd invited the Boys from Boulder to our much-glorified spring ritual.

Hands tucked into the front pockets of my jeans, I rocked back on the heels of my well-worn suede cowboy boots as I reminded my friend and fellow architect John that in addition to branding, the calves would be stripped of their natural, free behavior by the cowboys—a day when some of Boulder's more strident animal rights activists and vegetarians would have major issues. Just like in the movies, a calf's hide would be burned with hot red iron, forever tattooing the beast with cryptic cowboy hieroglyphics.

Our brand? Quarter-circle C slash.

I grabbed John's roll of bumwad tracing paper and drew the brand next to the flashing detail he'd been contemplating. We leaned over the drawing table and squinted at the two sketches. Cowboy versus architect—cattle country alongside tofu-loving Boulder.

A commodity with tangible value, in 1920 our brand traveled from Colorado to Wyoming. Subsequent to filing the appropriate paperwork, the brand transferred to us from Glenn. The flashing detail John had been perfecting might also be considered a commodity since we copyrighted construction documents, and the principal-in-charge signed and stamped—or branded—each page. Our firm owned those drawings. They could not be used without our permission.

I shrugged away the comparison and told John that this year's branding would be full-on cowboy! Rope and drag. Brand and shots and neuter. The cowboy way! We wanted to share the fun!

The Boys from Boulder rolled in on the Friday night before branding weekend, raising a commotion only matched by the rising plume of dust as they caravanned in—too fast—on our dirt road.

I escorted them through the fishing cabin to the newly constructed wooden deck hanging over the river, where barbecue smoke sifted into our nostrils. Hungry, we didn't hesitate to trade sightseeing for heaping plates of food, and after stuffing ourselves thoroughly with beef ribs, salad, and bread, we lingered on the deck, sipping beer after beer. We bitched about the office, the workload, and new code requirements, then shared our appreciation for the talented new interior designer. As the night cooled, our complaints flared as we dissected contractors who wanted us to do their job, to cover their asses and leave us holding the liability. We whined about demanding clients who wanted us to redesign their buildings for no fee and also be their bank since they never paid us on time.

Stars paved the Milky Way, and we relaxed into the night on the infamous drinking deck, shedding the pressures of our day jobs like

Wyoming rattlers writhing for release from too-tight skin. We listened to the chuckling river and laughed. And popped beer cans. And laughed. Hours past midnight, in that hazy, happy half-drunk stage, we all staggered to various cabins scattered across the ranch, then to bed.

Alarm clocks sounded before breaking daylight. I've never been hungry in the morning, and this morning my stomach felt as full as it had after I'd gorged on the barbecue ribs the night before. Beer full, reminding me of my college days. I ignored my discomfort and stepped into my tight jeans before padding into the bathroom. We needed an early start so we could finish before the heat of the day, which could stress the calves even more than we would with the roundup and branding. I wouldn't have minded another couple of hours of sleep, but no.

Yawning and stretching—plus more than one "Oh, my aching head"— my Boulder city slickers wandered into the kitchen to gulp coffee and grab sweet rolls or cereal. I finished my tea, and they obediently followed me down to the corral. Our ranch horses milled around, raising dust as they nudged each other out of the way to see who approached.

In the dim shed that doubled as one side of the corral, I grinned at some of my best friends. They'd all tried in vain to look like cowboys as I piled saddle blankets and unfamiliar tack into their arms. As is typical for most Boulder yuppies, every one of them enjoyed some sort of athletics, donning Lycra for biking or hiking and jogging, so they all looked fine in their jeans and jackets—but they didn't look like cowboys. New jeans, including fancy brands, and one pair even sported dry-cleaning creases down the front. Definitely *not* the cowboy way.

Like ducks gathering on a pond to snatch bread from the surface, the horses gathered around us. They sensed the excitement in the air. An early flake of hay, lights on before sunrise, and folks bustling around; our savvy ranch horses recognized the signs. They were going to work today. And so were the Boys from Boulder.

Our first order of business? Saddling a dozen horses—not just our six but the entire corral-full—so that when neighbors arrived later in the morning, mounts would be ready and waiting for them. I did most of the work, although Kirk caught on quickly; he saddled two to my three.

I showed David and Brad how to step up into their saddles and adjusted their stirrups to the right length. Kirk mounted. At ease on top of his horse, Kirk sat tall and flashed his quick grin, adjusted his baseball cap, and sidled close to hear my instructions. I'd worked with him for years and had no clue he could ride, not until that morning.

First I described the roundup, an urban cowboy's dream. We would gather 135 cows and 125 calves from one of several high prairie pastures on the west side of our land. Everyone's eyes glistened with excitement. I pushed my horse forward and leaned over to open the gate, leading the way to the wild, wild West.

Our ragtag posse of Boulder cowboys trailed behind, one effortlessly, others not, as they urged their horses forward, clicking their tongues or thumping the sides of their mount with their heels. I'd stopped to hold the gate, and as they passed, I told each the name of their horse. Tuff, Cyclone, Duke, Tiny, and Buddy. In accordance with typical cowboy humor, Cyclone had proved to be the calmest of the lot, and Tiny stood 16.5 hands, the tallest and fattest by far.

We clumped and slumped up the rocky, low-rising hill from the river-bottom corral to the upper pastures, with me providing pointers to the more overtly discomfited Boys. A couple of ranch hands from the neighboring spread rode up, their horses alert and warmed up, ready for action. I hoped I looked as comfortable in the saddle as they did, but my greetings were cut off when David's horse skittered sideways, not really spooked but feeling his oats and having some fun, showing off for the real cowboys. Horses are smart, and that ornery critter knew a novice rider had stepped into his saddle.

I didn't think Buddy would try to throw David but wanted to show him who was boss. The "real" cowboys saw David's dilemma, and advice peppered us, flowing as generously from the lips of those Wyoming cowboys as beer had flowed the night before on our drinking deck.

"Let that horse have his head, son. He knows what he's doing and you don't!"

"Don't worry about looking like a tinhorn—it's too late!"

"Grab hold of that saddle horn!"

"Push your heels down!"

"Better to look bad than slide off the rear end of your horse!"

Always a good sport, David ignored the red flush of embarrassment that claimed his neck and face as he adjusted his body. Save for Kirk, who needed no instruction, the Boys from Boulder listened and learned.

The edge of the sun peered at us from across the prairie, tinting the tall grass a reddish-orange. Off in the distance, black dots spread out across our land as far as we could see. Heads lowered to graze, cows and calves mowed the pasture. Beside me rode family and neighbors, friends and partners. Contentment saturated my every thought. I'd found my home, my future—as a cowboy.

We split up into three groups, blending experienced riders with novices, and as our horses spied our quarry—the distant cows—equine ears swiveled to point our way. Heads tossed. Heartbeats quickened. We had *work* to do!

Tuff, my old veteran of a gelding, had a ranching résumé that significantly outweighed my own. He'd spent his youth in the roping ring, lunging after long-legged calves, and I knew I'd need all of his talent and patience today. I kicked him into a trot and passed some of the Boulder Boys as they bounced and jounced in their saddles. Many a sore butt would be earned that day. I grinned and dug my heels into Tuff. We were off!

With my friends straggling behind and our experienced neighbors leading the way, we circled the scattered herd without overly alarming the calves.

Tuff ignored my rein commands more than once as we gathered and pushed about twenty reluctant pairs together. Initially the momma

THE BOYS FROM BOULDER

12. Riding Tuff, Bob West herds a steer prior to roping. Courtesy Bob West.

cows ignored us, enjoying their breakfast of new spring growth, a haze of green. Quietly we circled ever closer. That was the cowboy way—real cowboys knew it instinctively. Those of us from Boulder followed the softly spoken directions uttered by the Wyoming cowboys.

"There. Go left."

"No, don't trot. Keep it slow."

"Get behind that momma. She's gonna bolt."

The bawling and dust raised by over two hundred animals reminded me of a traffic jam in downtown Denver. Horns bellowed and tempers flared. One momma after another reluctantly acquiesced to our demands—though not without protest. Heat shimmered and dust danced in the air, clogging our throats.

As the remote teams of riders brought in more and more pairs, my newly christened cowboys from Boulder morphed naturally into the historic pattern of thousands of cattle drives. Forearms resting on saddle horns, hats or caps were lifted to wipe away sweat and grit. Momma cow bawled for baby and tried to U-turn around us. Escorted by a long-legged horse and rider, calves fled into the morass of black hides and swaying butts.

Our point rider, an experienced hand who worked for a neighbor, stayed near the front of the herd to guide us home. Other riders, called swing riders, swept the sides of the herd forward and back to contain the outermost pairs from making a run for it. Drag riders and flank riders, like Kirk and myself, rode at the back, eating dust, urging every man and animal forward. A determined calm settled. No panic.

Tuff, a trained drag rider horse, trotted easily along the back edge of the herd. We'd reach one side, and he'd spin around as if reading my mind, to trot to the other side. He put in miles and miles keeping that reluctant mass of black beef moving forward. I rode him, or perhaps I simply sat on him, as it was effortless on my part. That clever horse made me look good, and he made me feel good, as if we were one.

With the herd coaxed through the narrow gate at the corral, the real cowboys took over. Stiff and sore, the Boys from Boulder stepped down from their saddles, most staggering a pace or two before stopping to stretch. I did the same, stretching taut inner thigh and calf muscles. Bowlegged-ness came naturally to me—my legs curved slightly—and I'd ridden over the winter, so my muscles were tight but not sore. I knew my friends would be. Sitting in a cushioned office chair in front of a drawing board used a different set of muscles than those needed to scissor a 1,300-pound horse between your legs.

I watched as the real cowboys separated momma cows from calves in the twisting alleys of rusted steel and maze of gates. The bawling and bellowing escalated as calves cried out and mommas called back.

At about seven in the morning, more neighbors arrived, mostly young

13. Drag and flank riders during roundup on the Devil's Washtub Ranch.
Courtesy Bob West.

men exuding the scent of leather coated by Wyoming dust. Ropers in
hefty, red pickup trucks stepped down proudly from their Detroit steel,
Knights of the Round Table ready to joust. One such knight, name
of Richer, caught my eye. He backed his already-saddled horse from
his battered two-horse trailer, flipped the reins over the horse's neck,
and mounted him with such lithe ease that I thought of the fluidity of
an Olympic diver. Richer's tall silhouette against the backdrop of the
morning sun would have made Clint Eastwood envious. I grinned. No
surprise that everyone from Boulder swiveled their heads in unison to
watch Richer ride up to the corral gate. At least the women were subtle
with their casual glances, as opposed to the men, who stared with eyes
and mouths wide open.

Like a panther roaring over his kill, the branding fire ignited—a signal
for the veteran cowboys and horses. That propane-fed roar of flames became constant background noise as we made ready to *really* get to work.

Inside the corral we paired off into teams of two wranglers, or wrestlers, who would handle the calves after the ropers snared and dragged the calves by their hind legs close to the fire. "Rope and drag"—it looked easy to my virgin cowhands.

A roper, Richer in fact, quietly rode into the mass of bawling calves, backed into a huddle in the far corner of the corral. Richer isolated one calf and cut it from the herd, horse dancing and turning without any apparent commands. A rope loop blossomed beneath the calf's heels. I'd blinked and missed Richer's throw, but I did see the calf step into the loop. Richer paused for a moment, then flicked the stiff rope. The loop closed around both legs of the calf. The calf stumbled as Richer dallied the rope around his saddle horn while his horse pivoted toward the waiting team of wranglers, dragging the struggling calf behind.

I watched the pros for a few minutes, quickly deciding that I needed a large, strong partner and that the potential for injury was focused primarily on the rear wrangler as thrashing rear hooves often tap danced against a wrangler's chest and stomach. So I took the front position and waved over Brad as my partner—a six-foot-three, 220-pound weight-lifting friend from Boulder. He didn't have any experience, but by God, he had muscles. And he almost looked the part, inspiring at least a modicum of confidence.

Our first calf.

Our team on center stage.

Brad grabbed the rope a half dozen or so feet behind the calf and gave it a yank, but the critter didn't budge. Now what? I instinctively grabbed the steer's thick black neck and tried to flank the calf by picking up his front legs. A classic battle of man versus beast followed, and between us tugging and twisting, we finally got him down. A decent start. Not great, but decent.

Half kneeling, I jumped across that calf's neck, and now Brad needed to grasp the totally pissed-off animal's rear legs so we could stretch the body out between us. Unfortunately our two-hundred-pound calf had only been roped by one leg. Hooves flailed, and one narrowly missed

14. Drawn after a few beers at day's end, a sketch of 1998 branding efforts on the Devil's Washtub Ranch. Sketch by Kirk Hale, courtesy Bob West.

Brad's skull. Grunting, he got hold of one black leg but wasn't quick enough to grab the second. He rolled forward and sort of laid across the rear end of the animal, then reached under his own body to grab the other rear leg. Grip secured, he loosened the rope, so the roper and his horse could back away.

Panting, we held down that bucking, bawling critter. Seeing close up what happened next, I fully understood why he fought so hard.

Two women, both neighbors, leaned in to poke him in the neck with two different needles. These weren't delicate little needles. A grizzled old cowboy approached, bucket held low in one hand, clean blade held firmly in the other, and nodded at Brad to spread the calf's legs apart. One flick of that knife and off came a tiny pair of balls. I flinched. Then another cowgirl swabbed the open wound with antiseptic. Yikes! I knew when I spoke again, the pitch of my voice would have raised at least an octave. Pills were poked down the calf's throat while yet another ranching tradition unfolded before us as an older neighbor named Stumbaugh wielded the branding iron. Only those with years of experience and the squint lines to prove it would lay gloved hands on that oh-so-hot iron.

A flare of flames and the bitter smoke from burning calf hair and hide filled my lungs as a miniature earthquake erupted beneath my hands. Finally with the critter's horn buds burned away, I nodded at Brad, and in unison we released our grips to step away from the calf.

Trembling, the critter staggered to his feet, moaned, shook his head, then scurried back to hide with the waiting victims at the end of the corral. Brad flexed his right hand. Only one hundred and forty to go.

I did notice a new phenomenon after we tackled our next calf. Both Brad and I kept our legs clenched tight when that knife approached. Instinct, I think.

With only a few minor wrecks, such as when a calf twisted free, turning the rope into a potential decapitation device, our branding moved right along. A couple of calves maintained enough footing to give one of the Boys from Boulder a ride, akin to mutton busting at a rodeo when a six-year-old soon-to-be cowboy would cling desperately to thick wool and race around the arena. No broken bones. No black eyes. For beast *or* man.

Panting for breath after wrangling seven calves, Brad and I stepped back so Tucker and Kirk could take their turn. We watched in awe as Kirk expertly downed their first calf with a fancy twist of the rope. He pointed Tucker to the front of the critter and told him where to lean against the calf's neck. Branding and inoculations completed in record time, Kirk nodded at Tucker and they jumped up. Kirk wasn't even dusty! That sometimes shy, laughing partner of mine—an incredible design talent—had been holding out on me! Kirk caught my eye, flashed his Tom Selleck smile, doffed his baseball cap, then waded back in to topple the next calf.

15. Bob West grabs the rope prior to wrestling a calf to the ground for branding. Courtesy Bob West.

With work now complete for everyone except the wranglers and ropers, the rancher's wives laid out the traditional post-branding spread atop rented fold-down tables in our garage shop, usually home to John Deere tractors and haying equipment.

After my third stint at wrangling, I turned my gaze onto those tables laden with ham, potato salad, and mounds of frothy salad. The sweet molasses aroma of baked beans and bacon overcame the scent of burning hair, and my mouth watered. I'd been up since dawn, burned thousands of calories, and my stomach was a hole.

We chatted and shared tall tales until the last of the branded calves bounded back to his brethren. With the hiss of the extinguished branding fire acting in lieu of a dinner bell, we lined up for a quick wash before forming a line at the shop.

Shaking my head but without time to intervene, I watched Ellen, our architectural firm's marketing director, queue up at the front of the long line of buffet-style fixings. As she reached for the stack of paper plates, a half-pint youth—a ten- or twelve-year-old boy clad in jeans, boots, and dusty black Stetson—stepped pointedly in front of her, looked her in the eyes, and said, "Ma'am, the cowboys eat first." Polite but firm, cowboy culture steeped in long-held tradition clashed with the young urbanite. Ellen flushed scarlet and backed away, as did Katie, who'd been in line right behind her.

The next day Jake told us that one of our heifer calves died sometime around midnight. He thought the calf might have been weakened by the stress of branding and moving the herd, and the coyotes got her. While *we* enjoyed the physical challenges of branding, we'd set up the critter to fail. Made me stop and think.

19. MURPHY'S LAW

I came up alone on Friday night so our ranch hand could leave for vacation. Alone on thousands of acres. Alone except for a dozen horses, a few dogs, 150 pairs of black angus, and who knows how many wild critters. I kept my fingers crossed and uttered a few silent prayers against Murphy and his ubiquitous law.

Katie and the boys came up Saturday morning, and almost at once, Murphy laughed. Out loud. More than once.

First our neighbors called. Our new bull decided to go courting, uninvited, to visit the lovely ladies next door. That cocky beast must have kicked his heels up at us a half dozen times as we tried in vain to herd him back through the gap he'd made in the barbwire fence. Next morning the drool-inducing rattle of a bucket of cake brought him running along with three calves. Fortunately that delinquent trio also bore our brand.

We patched the hole in the fence with twists of wire and well-placed rocks.

On our way back to the cabin, we stumbled across a dead calf on the east side of the road. With an intact carcass and no signs of illness, I wondered if lightning during the previous night's thunderstorm could be blamed. Nothing else made sense.

Begone, Murphy.

Dragging the corpse to the dead pile, where we heaped the remains of critters for coyotes and other scavengers to feast on, wasn't the most pleasant of chores. In spite of the stench and any sorrow I might harbor over the loss of one of our calves, it always reminded me of the circle of life.

The following Friday, the let's-help-Bob-while-Jake-is-on-vacation baton passed from Katie, who was off to California to see her father, to Tucker and Rachel. A gentle breeze cooled the night, as did the beers we enjoyed on the drinking deck. Stars overwhelmed the sky, making our quest to spot falling stars somewhat challenging. So did the fourth or fifth round of beers.

I prayed yet again that nothing beyond our experience level would come calling.

At Jake's cabin the next morning, I showed Tucker the instructions for feeding Odie, Jake's dog, along with our ranch hand's invisible cat. The feline food always disappeared, and I never saw Odie sniff the fishy stuff, so my notion of invisibility had some validity, though perhaps not much.

Odie, companion to the invisible cat, had his own strange traits. In fact I wouldn't have blinked had he been named Oddball.

The day I met Odie, I knew that he was a natural-born top dog, albeit a confused one. An Aussie, a breed that herds by barking and nipping at a cow's heels, rather than the pure, body-flattened, pause 'n' trot sideways stealth of the border collie, Odie always got the job done, at least when it came to cattle.

Odie lived to ride on the ranch truck. He would leap on top of bales of hay stacked three high in the bed of the truck—and I'm talking a single leap from ground to the top bale, not like some circus performer climbing a ladder. Then that dog would stand stiff-legged, nose pointed forward, on lookout as my ranch hand's battered blue pickup truck rock 'n' rolled across Wyoming's barren fields.

The only dog I ever met that would growl while his nub of a tail and hind end wagged an enthusiastic "hello," I always wondered whether Odie wanted to kiss me or bite me. Guess it depended on the day, and he liked to keep his options open. I also wondered if Odie had been kicked in the head once too often by some angry momma cow defending her calf, or wasn't given enough affection by my ranch hand—a man who used animals as animals as opposed to pampered pets, although I didn't believe he'd knowingly mistreat one. Regardless that dog pretty much loved Jake to death.

Sadly that love wasn't reciprocated when Jake and his wife received one too many complaints about Odie's threatening growl, topped by breeding, unasked, a neighbor's young pup—one too young to be having her own pups. Conceding defeat, Jake gave Odie away. Hauled him into town. Banished a top dog to sidewalks and leashes. Two weeks later, grinning an embarrassed doggy grin, footsore from his eighteen-mile marathon, good ol' Odie trotted up to Jake's back door, wagging and growling as if to say, "You didn't really mean it, did you? Me? Live in town? You've got to be kidding. I'm a working dog. A top dog!"

Jake did mean it, and Odie disappeared soon after. I never could find it in my heart to ask where Odie had gone on his last trip in Jake's pickup truck. But it could have been to say goodbye as he looked down a .30-06 barrel. I really didn't want to know.

That is one thing I both dislike *and* respect about many ranch and farm folks. They don't romanticize animals. Either the beast is useful or it's not, and if not, you deal with it. Personally. Mercy will invariably find the animal's end swift and painless, but I couldn't have pulled the trigger on Odie. Odd he might have been, perhaps even demented, but he loved life. And he loved the ranch and doing his own small part to help herd our cattle. I hope Odie's standing atop bales of hay in some pickup truck right now, swaying as rocks and gullies rise up beneath soft tires, his nose pointed into the wind, searching for wayward cattle over the next horizon, and with a pat of the hand for a job well done.

20. INDEPENDENCE DAY!

After feeding all the close-in critters, we drove out to check the cows grazing near our prairie dog village. Out of the blue, Tucker decided that he wanted to shoot him a prairie dog. Over my objections he loaded his pistol, blasted away, and missed! Lucky dogs!

While his impromptu fireworks didn't prod us to head into Wheatland for the fireworks, he did suggest we attend the patriotic small-town show at the fairgrounds, brim with singing, laughter, and sticky-with-cotton-candy kids.

A finger tap on the microphone brought us all to attention, and with every cap or hat removed, we joined together in singing our National Anthem, whether off-tune or not. Parents snagged overexcited young ones to hold them close and quieted them with hands held over their hearts.

Bright big eyes stared solemnly as the flag, attached to a chain at the base of the flagpole, snapped in the light breeze as the mayor pulled the chain hand over hand, lifting the flag to the tip-top of the pole as our small-town chorale blended patriotism with song, respect for freedom, and our flag.

Oh, so proud, I sang along. These tough and independent people understood and embraced sacrifice for family, for freedom, for country.

As our final note joined the flag in the sky, a huge red firework blossomed in the heights. Then another. We oohed and aahed with everyone, shook dozens of hands, and shared gossip where offered.

Folks in Wheatland treated us with grace, though we would likely always be "Greenies"—defined by the color of our vehicle plates rather than an environmental moniker. Nor would the ranch ever be considered "our place" or even the Devil's Washtub Ranch. Instead it would forever and always be described as the Harrison Ranch.

Rachel thought everyone in town and the surrounding ranches might have traveled to the fairgrounds for the festivities, though we didn't spot Glenn or Martha. I decided to stop by to say hello next time I stayed at the ranch without Katie.

Subterfuge? Nope. Simply keeping the peace.

Saturday morning after we fed the horses and Jake's invisible cat, we of course went to check on the cows. All too soon we discovered another hole in the fence near Shockley's cottonwoods. Four of our calves had wandered into the shade beneath the trees, close to a bunch of Shockley's cows. On foot we tried to herd our delinquent quartet back through the gap and managed instead to rile up some of the cows, and they bolted through the opening onto our property. Talk about great cowboys! Where were our sticks when we needed them?

After more than a few sweaty, curse-laden minutes, we gave up and headed over to Shockley's house. On the way we found our wandering bull, that devil.

At about four miles' distance, Shockley was our closest neighbor. A multi-generational Wyoming rancher, he'd always been willing to lend a hand and share his expertise. A quiet man, he and his wife, whom we rarely spoke to, appeared to live quite frugally.

Somehow Shockley managed to keep a straight face as he pulled fence repair equipment from his pickup bed, choreographed our movements to sort out the cows and calves, personally guided the bull back onto our property, and mended the gap in the fence. That old cowboy made it all look so easy.

How many miles of fence would it take for me to achieve that level of ease?

After all the commotion, I went for a ride by myself. Down in the central pasture I paused to lean on my saddle horn and watch a thunderstorm roll in. As the clouds blossomed upward, layer upon layer, I pondered the level of respect I held for true cowboys and whether my own actions, whether my life and values, echoed theirs. Why I wanted all of that.

Respecting the land, caring for animals, and most importantly, cherishing family, friends, and community—I did all of that, always had.

To cowboy up didn't mean strutting around with spurs jingle-jangling; it meant embracing your life and livelihood with modesty, admitting and apologizing for wrongs while inspiring others to do *their* best. I hoped I did all of that, always, here *and* with our architectural firm. Cowboys like Shockley inspired me to do better, to emulate their every nuance, even when they had to be laughing at the quasi-tinhorns living next door.

I grinned at my own ineptitude as the storm grumbled my way, announcing its true power with a pair of lightning bolts spearing from the heights to hit the ground about three miles distant. Being the tallest thing on the prairie made me a target, so I straightened and urged my horse to skedaddle back to the barn. We galloped home.

Later that afternoon, when the rain had cooled our hot July daytime temperature by at least ten degrees, Tucker padded through the kitchen dressed in Lycra jogging shorts and shirt, carrying his running shoes. Out to the mailbox and back he went, and I suspect the bulls and cows watched in amazement as he pounded by, getting in his miles.

After he'd cooled off from his run, we jumped into the red ranch pickup truck for our evening check on the cows. I laughed out loud when we spied yet another calf running up and down the fence line on Shockley's property, his momma pacing him on our side of the fence. Long story short, we disassembled the repair of the gap in the fence, drove through, and—with much waving out the windows and a toot of the horn—herded the calf through the gap. An hour later, after repairing the fence a second time, I almost felt like a real cowboy. Almost. I might have if we'd been on horseback!

INDEPENDENCE DAY!

Dusk of that long day found us out on the drinking deck, cracking open a fresh bottle of Scotch. Below us a merganser momma duck leading her brood cut through the river shallows as if aligned by a straight edge. Those ducklings had more sense than our calves, and the previous day we'd even seen a few ducklings riding their momma's back as she waddled along the shore. No fools, those ducklings, sticking close.

One more day with Jake on vacation found me grooming all of our riding horses after morning feeding. They loved me, or more likely, the brushes, shifting to lean into the bristles when I reached a particular itch. I loved them too but didn't like that I could see ribs on most of them. I've owned horses for a long time and tend to pamper them, and while extra weight isn't necessarily good, I didn't want to stint on feed. Keeping an eye on expenses is good, but grain doesn't cost that much, so I made a note to talk to Jake.

I also found a few spots of fresh blood on JC's hoof, but the cut looked like it had closed up. Decided to call the vet anyway, just to be sure.

Midday we thought we'd take a picnic lunch up to the Washtub, and the ground gave way beneath our front tires where the road goes through the washout on the far side of the river. Gave us a pretty good jolt, and my red truck clunked in protest. Yet another task for Jake—regrading. He was going to wish he stayed on vacation once he read my to-do list.

21. BULL RIDER

Katie headed north early to paint some of the finished walls in the new cabin, and I drove up with the boys after work. Katie's friend Giles and Frank "the accountant" caravanned up with us. We quickly settled them into the lower cabin, and when the normally sedate duo spotted the river, everyone laughed at their declarations to fish all weekend. On Sunday night Dad and Mom, Smokey and Doris, and Butch and Sandra all arrived to stay the week. With ten adults and our effervescent boys stepping on everyone else's toes between the three cabins, I couldn't help but yearn for completion of the log cabin we were building on the old foundation near the river. Soon.

After Katie and I sealed drywall in the bedrooms of the new cabin, we left our stress behind by fishing for a few hours, then saddled horses to ride up near the Washtub where the remnants of tepee circles still tattoo our land.

Glenn's enviable and museum-grade arrowhead collection had been assembled over two lifetimes, so our modest basket of broken flint and knapping stones had quite a way to go. We knew we'd never catch up, but we enjoyed tramping around in hopes of discovering perfect, unbroken examples of that ancient craft.

I whooped when I spotted what looked to be a faultless arrowhead. Greenish gray and as long as my thumb, it had been half buried in dirt, but when I gently pried it free, I couldn't help but share my excitement.

After rubbing the slick flint completely free of dirt, I handed it first to my younger son, Paul. When Paul relinquished our treasure to his brother Shawn, I asked my boys if they thought it had been attached to a wooden shaft and lost in a hunt.

Eyes shining, they nodded in tandem. Even though that still-sharp

16. Sketch of new cabin. Courtesy Bob West.

17. New cabin. Courtesy Bob West.

arrowhead could have easily been lost while unpacking or packing a camp, I dropped to my knees next to my sons and pulled them close. Suggesting they close their eyes, I described my vision of what a temporary settlement of a dozen or so families of Oglala Sioux might have looked like two hundred years before.

The scent of pinion smoke would rise from eight or ten cook fires, burning not too far from the tepees. Young boys the age of Paul and Shawn might have slipped down to the Washtub to fill water bags made of buffalo stomachs or to spear the large snapping turtles that sunned themselves on the rocks. Bearing their prizes, the boys would strut into camp so the turtles could roast for supper or an early morning meal.

Horses would graze nearby.

Women would be busy tending their babies, scraping hides, cleaning fish or small game.

Some of the men might be crouched on nearby boulders, keeping watch, or possibly even knapping flint—the very arrowhead my boys passed back and forth.

Turning that arrowhead over and over in their hands, the boys studied every edge, every curve of a chip struck from the base stone. Handing it back to me, first one, then the other, nodded solemnly before dashing off to look for more.

When we got back to the cabins, Jake and Hallie stopped by to warn us they'd killed a twelve-button rattlesnake in the east pasture. A snakebite from a rattler that big might kill one of the boys. Hell, it could kill an adult. We needed to remind everyone to listen for that shivering, dry rattle of warning and to avoid reaching into dark crevices, especially by the woodpiles.

Jake then shared another piece of bad news. He'd found a four-hundred-pound dead calf, one born in March. Couldn't tell what had happened to him, which made me imagine the worst. We'd need to keep a close eye on the herd in case a contagion of some sort had come calling.

Another week, another dollar. Make that thirty thousand dollars for a 310E John Deere skid steer. We wrote checks for this place faster than the Laramie River flowed off our property. Faster than a Chinook wind. Faster than . . . never mind. My better-than-average salary groaned under the weight of those checks. Thankfully Katie's father didn't mind writing some of the larger ones, though I didn't like asking for his contributions. Pride? No doubt. But no way around it.

We ferried up the light fixtures for the new cabin only to discover Brian hanging the doors—he'd already completed installing the cabinets. They looked great. Brian also bragged that he caught a nineteen-inch trout up the canyon. I would have loved to have seen that fish. Better yet, I want to catch that fish's twin brother!

We had work to do, but how I enjoyed it, especially after sitting at my desk all week. We put up 364 bales of hay by Friday night and another 124 bales on Saturday, then, after a cursory wash, hurried over to the Platte County Fair to watch Jake compete in the bull riding contest.

Bull riders are daring and strong and fast and at least half a bubble off plumb. I mean that as a compliment. No bull!

Soon after we settled onto some of the rough wood bench seats, they announced Jake would be riding Humphrey the bull. Now this county fair didn't offer prize money or fame to the winners of bull riding at rodeos like Cheyenne Frontier Days, but our local cowboys signed up to ride those bulls, I think, not only for the notoriety but primarily to prove something to themselves.

A bucking bull is usually a Brahma, typically crossed with another breed, and those big boys weigh in at 1,800 pounds or more. I don't think Jake weighed 170, even with his boots on.

When the gate slapped open, Humphrey plunged sideways, trying to flip Jake into the gate. When that maneuver failed, the beast jumped forward and turned into a tilt-o-whirl, throwing Jake off balance and planting him in the wall. As Jake caught his breath, Humphrey tried to gore our hired hand, but today's event only used bulls whose horns had been removed, thank goodness! Before Jake could pull himself to the top of the fence, Humphrey returned and tried to stomp on Jake but missed.

What fun.

No bull. Not for me, thank you very much.

Despite his bruises, both physical and to his ego, or maybe *because of* his ego, over the next week Jake finished the haying without us—1,400 bales, 400 more than last year. He also sold our big bull. Apt timing, considering his wild Brahma ride, but I didn't mention that to him. Anyway, the bull came in at 1,610 pounds, so we received a check for $679.04 after deductions for feed, yardage fee, and market charge. Another spit in the bucket.

Tucker beat us up to the ranch for once to help Tim "the Tin Man" put up the patterned tin we were using in the kitchen. Fred finished installing the carpet for only $350—a bargain. We needed to finish the stairs and railing and hook up the HVAC and propane. Then our new home would be done! The first house I designed *and* built for myself. Sweet.

Next up our steers and heifers went to auction. Average weight of 472 pounds resulted in about $438 for each steer and $395 per heifer. That helped nourish our always-hungry checking account.

The twenty heifers we kept to build our herd looked well-matched and sturdy. With winter on our event horizon, I didn't want any delicate animals in our corrals.

Since they weren't insulated for winter weather, I asked Jake to go ahead and shut down the fishing cabins. We'd stay in the new cabin from now on. Sure enough a blizzard closed I-25 North in the third week of October, and we had eight inches of snow in Boulder. As always the weather turned nasty just before Halloween.

In November we went to Torrington to close on forty acres of haying and grazing land for $19,000. This small section of land adjacent to our ranch could only be accessed through our property, and the three old freight cars, sans tracks, had been used as camping shelters for the annual orphanage camping trip. No one could remember how or when the cars rolled onto the parcel, and we didn't plan on rolling them off.

That same day we received the bill for timber for the new bridge. $10,000. Easy come, easy go. Let me rephrase that. Easy go, easy go.

22. FEEDING TIME!

Black angus aren't stupid, but they're not exactly smart either. Though bred as domesticated animals, during the warmest part of the year they are savvy enough to be left on their own to graze the vast Wyoming prairie.

Using it solely as an excuse for a ride, I would regularly saddle a horse to head out to check on the herd. Countless artists have tried to capture what I enjoyed in real life. Atop a low ridge I'd rein to a stop, lean forward on my saddle horn, and fall silent to gaze across a serene valley capped by the bluest of skies. No people. No cars. No telephones or billboards or buildings.

My horse would stretch his neck, tugging to loosen my hold on his reins so he could lower his head and graze. The stress of my day job, of deadlines and staffing and budgets and taxes, fell from my shoulders to be absorbed by this arid yet fertile land.

Below or over yonder, when tired of grazing, calves played their own version of tag, romping around their mommas whose focus remained primarily on ripping up mouthfuls of brome and fescue, though they also glanced around regularly to watch for predators. Chewing thoughtfully, when they spotted me or my horse, they stared. I wonder if they thought I had buckets of cow cake hidden out of sight? Or were they waiting for other cowboys to appear, to start urging them to other pastures or into a branding corral?

My gaze scanned the horizon with theirs as I contemplated whether any big cats lounged in the shadows, studying each of the smaller angus to see if any weakness might slow their step or hinder sharp hooves.

There were no fences to segregate the inhabitants of much of this high prairie, and I could easily envision a mass of dusty buffalo grazing this open range instead of our shiny black beasts. In fact the "Open Range" sign on Fletcher Park Road, which divided our largest and primary pasture, had been used for target practice by many a cowboy. I doubted city slickers, other than ourselves early on and more recently our friends and family, had ever seen land such as this—where cattle can roam, unhindered, for many months of the year.

Winter tells a different tale.

When the brittle November winds turn pastures brown, little nutritional value remains in those husks of grass. November, of course, is critical for mommas. They need additional weight—fat—to sustain the six- to seven-month-old fetus they're carrying and keep their own body temperature constant through rugged Wyoming winters. November heralds the beginning of daily feeding.

It's one thing to wander into your warm kitchen to fill your dog's shiny aluminum bowl with wholesome dog food twice a day, and another, a polar opposite, in fact, to feed a herd of cattle, especially if winter winds are sweeping down from the Arctic.

Daily adventures abound.

Those adventures lured my sons to rise at first light, never an easy accomplishment for them when at home in Boulder. On the ranch they could actually help without getting trampled, run over, or falling from the heights. Mostly.

After helping my youngest son zip up his wind pants and parka, tug on cowboy boots, and making sure both boys had their gloves, my miniature ranchers followed me outside. They'd climb into the cab of our ranch truck as I cranked over the cold engine, then I'd hop back out to scrape ice off the windshield.

Off we'd roar to the "cow cake" storage shed—if roaring is defined as five, maybe ten miles per hour. With the smell of vitamins permeating the area, if a particularly cold morning, the truck would remain running while we tramped inside the shed to face the seven-foot-high mound of three-inch-long pellets that might save a human's life during an apocalypse, though I didn't want to bite into one. Beet pulp, corn, other grains, vitamins, and minerals—a candy bar for cows!

With all of us wielding shovels, filling six five-gallon plastic buckets took only moments, then the boys loaded the buckets into the contraption claiming the bed of the truck. That mechanism, a delivery system for the pellets, saved us a great deal of effort. Once loaded, and usually with one of my sons steering the truck from my lap, we'd head to the lower pasture gate where the smart cows gathered every morning at exactly the same time. I could have set a clock by them.

It took all of us to keep the cattle on their side of the fence as we opened the gate wide enough for the truck to ease through. Enthusiasm for morning breakfast created a logjam of noisy, shoving critters, but once I'd edged into their space, the boys would close the gate and then jump into the bed of the truck.

Surrounded by a sea of black hides, I'd feather the gas pedal until we broke out into open pasture where I could speed up.

Breakfast is served!

Pulling a rope threaded through the driver's side window, I'd hold the truck at an even pace in a straight line. Cake fell to the ground in a well-spaced constant pattern. Running wildly after the truck, the first of the cows would skid to a stop at the closest cake, with the next stopping and pivoting at the second cake. Soon a football field length of cake had been evenly distributed, every black angus with their own ration.

One morning after significant chomping noises had replaced the thunder of hooves, I heard my oldest son yelling as he pounded on the back window. I looked in the rearview mirror. Shit. I'd lost my youngest son.

I rolled to a stop and jumped out of the cab with visions of a seriously injured boy trampled by heavy hooves.

Calling his name, I pushed through the cows, my older son following.

There! Paul pushed himself up to a sitting position. Curious mommas circled this strange thing in the field, but far more interested in eating than son-gazing, they trotted down the line of cake looking for another tasty treat.

Paul's face said it all. He had no idea what he was doing on the ground.

He looked around, at me, his approaching brother, and a multitude of black angus legs and butts.

As he started pushing himself to his feet, I leaned over to hold his shoulders so he'd remain sitting. "'M okay," he muttered. As I asked questions about various body parts and vision and aches, he kept shaking his head.

Youth, a strong body, and what sounded like a somersault off the truck saved the day. He'd probably be sore, but I was a different kind of sore at myself for not taking better care driving over the ruts and rocks. After dusting him off we threaded our way through the cows. By the time we reached the truck, he acted as if this had been an acrobatic adventure worthy of a circus performance. I, on the other hand, wondered how many gray hairs might have joined me.

We all climbed into the truck bed to do the count. Butts up, heads down, all in a row, how many cows had joined in the synchronized eating this morning? Glenn could do the count in about three minutes, and while I was getting better at it, I needed to improve. A special skill, I later figured out the secret.

Counting 150 black cows, necessary so we'd know all of the cows were healthy and accounted for, took speed. If you counted too slowly, cows at the beginning of the line that had eaten first trotted on down to see if there were any unclaimed cake treats. If I didn't get started right away, when I hit 123, 124, 125 . . . oh, shit . . . down the row they trotted. Time to start the count again.

With numbers running through my mind, I crawled back into the cab of the truck, waited for the boys to join me, then headed back to ranch headquarters to pick up the green (of course) John Deere 4440 tractor. With its heated cab, big enough for a driver and a couple of boys, we didn't get too chilled as I drove to the round bale hay storage area, backed the tractor to a bale, made sure the two three-foot-long parallel spikes were positioned correctly, and speared a 1,200-pound bale. That big ol' tractor picked up the eight-foot-wide bale like it was a 75-pound dog.

18. Bob West removing baling twine from a round bale. Courtesy Bob West.

Back we headed to the gate and cows, most of which had finished their appetizers and were anxious for the main course.

Now came what might be a balancing act or minor magic trick.

With orange bailing twine removed, when tipped off the tractor spears, that bale of hay would roll out in a long strip of hay like a magic carpet. But the twine would kill a cow, slowly and painfully, if ingested.

First I had to remove most of the twine while on our side of the gate. Too much, and the bale would fall apart before I made it through the gate. We repeated our open-the-gate and edge through the mass of angus, many of which would try to start eating from the bale while still held by the tractor.

I'd trundle forward twenty or thirty feet, leap from the cab, cut the remaining twine, and pull hard to get it loose from the bottom of the bale.

Back in the cab, and hopefully without running over an early diner, I lowered the bale to the ground. If done correctly, it rolled out in a

19. Bob West in a tractor, rolling out hay for the herd. Courtesy Bob West.

continuous strip, so the hungry herd could line up on either side and chow down.

I became fairly proficient at all of this, and aside from losing Paul off the truck that one time, I only had one other mishap, one that made me so sick and miserable that I never confessed my mistake until now.

Early on in our ranching days, one morning as I pulled the last strands of twine from the bale before rolling it out, a young heifer chomped on a mouthful of hay *and* twine and swallowed. Chomped again and swallowed. I scrabbled around the hay to grab that twine, only to see it slurped up like spaghetti by that hungry eating machine.

Shit. Shit. Shit.

The next day taught me an excruciating lesson—one that still makes my gut hurt and heart ache. My rookie mistake cost that young animal her life as the twine sliced her insides into pieces like wire carving cheese. I can't bear to imagine the pain she felt those last few hours.

Ranching is a serious business. Life or death. It was on me.

23. A RED-TAILED HAWK

Whenever I had a few minutes to pause on top of the butte above the lower fishing cabin, I'd fallen into the habit of spying on one of our new neighbors, a red-tailed hawk. After perusing the landscape from high, this elegant raptor decided to build a nest in one of the tallest pines on the south side of the river.

From the butte you could peer down into her nest, and we celebrated the day we spotted three large white eggs nestled amid woven twigs, clumps of grass, and tufts of feathers. A review of a book on local birds taught me that red-tails mated for life, quite an accomplishment in this world of brief marriages and fear of commitment.

Once the chicks hatched, we set up the telescope at the cabin so we could watch the daily progress of our feathered family. On a windy day in June a single white, down-covered, gangly head appeared above the edge of the nest, and for the remainder of that afternoon we took turns at the telescope, counting the minutes until two, and then all three eggs successfully hatched.

In less than a day the parents' pace escalated. Hungry beaks waving above the edge of the stick and feathered fortress? We spotted snakes, toads, rabbits, fish, prairie dogs, and mice lifted onto the edge of the nest by the sharp talons of the male and female hawk. Then with surgical precision, mom or dad's beak sliced the tasty treat into bite-sized pieces before sharing it among the young'uns.

Day after day, the male raptor and slightly larger female alternated between guard duty and swooping into the nest with yet another meal. Rattlesnakes proved to be particularly entertaining.

Talons wrapped firmly around the body of the snake, the hawk would first land in a nearby tree. As the snake continued to coil and try to wrap itself around the legs and body of the red-tail, the bird would reposition its hold, sometimes jumping back into the air briefly to avoid a strike or to loosen the rattler's hold. The bird's head dipped regularly to strike at the snake, and minutes into this deadly dance, and once positioned correctly, the hawk repeatedly whipped or pinned the head of the snake against the tree trunk.

A few beaky kisses later, that limp, lifeless snake would then be airlifted to the nest, where the snake would be filleted into bite-sized morsels.

Days passed, and with the gore of feeding came flies and other insects to harass the young birds. Chores followed soon after, mom and dad showing the chicks how to throw bones and leftover body parts out of the nest.

Two of the chicks grew at a faster rate than the third, less aggressive youngster. At feeding time, the dynamic duo shoved their smaller sibling behind them, so meals weren't proportional, though mom and dad endeavored to feed all three.

As slick, handsome feathers replaced their soft white down, hawkish facial features emerged, along with demands for even more food as the chicks grew to about two-thirds of adult size. Perching on the side of the nest to stretch their wings wide, the trio appeared anxious to take flight.

Never able to cope with death and with my mother in hospice, I sought refuge at the ranch. On a beautiful Sunday morning capped by intense blue skies and white cotton clouds, loud shrieks—red-tailed hawk shrieks—pierced the silence. A few minutes later, while listening to a message on the ranch phone that cancer had claimed my mother's life, I found myself shivering as I wondered whether the hawk shrieks had been bird calls at all but instead loudspeakers from heaven.

Mom delighted in spying on the young birds through the telescope during her final visit to the ranch. Later in the hospital, I would invariably be blessed by her smile when I reported on the progress of the growing hawks. She never complained about the misery of side effects as she submitted to lengthy treatment without pause, though those of us that loved her could count the daily toll. I hurried to pack, to help my brother, sister, and father make arrangements for a celebration of her life.

As I stepped out on the porch to lock the door, the gentlest of rain touched my face, and framed by the smudge of a newly born rainbow, I spied three young hawks gliding oh so effortlessly in the thermals. They screeched for their parents or for the joy of flight or to simply stake their claims to the sky; I don't know which or why. Their loud proclamations of freedom—of great spirit—swept across the entire valley as the spirit of my mother joined them in the heights, crossing over to a better place.

24. BUFFALO DANCE

Every thousand years people gather to celebrate the end, and beginning, of a millennium. The new year of 2000 presented us with exactly that opportunity at the ranch. Worldwide celebrations included opulent fireworks, concerts, and masses of people dancing in the street. Our ranch celebration, planned in secret by Tucker and Rachel, found us rendezvousing at the upper cabin at 10:00 p.m. after they arrived from Denver.

Dutifully and with anticipation, we enjoyed walking up to the cabin on this calm, moonlit night. The tenacious Wyoming winds decided to drowse on this cold December evening—Wheatland's news agencies reported we'd had a dry autumn with rare snow.

No one answered the door when we knocked, but we knew they'd arrived as their car was parked alongside the cabin. So as was our norm, we walked on in, calling, "Hello." A mound of Native blankets, animal skins, and pots of black, red, and white face paint sat in the middle of the living room, topped by a note—written instructions directing us to help the boys paint streaks of color across their foreheads and cheeks, and for all of us to wrap ourselves in the robes or blankets. Bemused, we followed their instructions, though the boys insisted Katie and I paint stripes on our cheeks, as well.

The final instruction told us to head out to the woodpile for long sticks, five to six feet in length, and sharpen one end to emulate a spear. A modest bouquet of feathers, supposedly from owls, provided one feather per spear, which we were to strap near the sharpened point. We were then to travel to the new cabin, finished earlier that month. Gracing the banks of the North Laramie River in the valley, our new abode had gained the infinitely appropriate honorific of "the lower cabin."

Traveling by truck now, a boisterous bonfire guided us to our destination. Clad in similar robes and brandishing their own spears, Tucker and Rachel stepped out of the shadows. Whooping with excitement, the boys leaped from the truck, only to skid to a stop as Tucker solemnly held up his hands to greet them.

After waving us close to the fire, he related that the tribes that'd first inhabited this land, including the acres comprising our ranch, hunted many animals. Tonight as a spiritual white man's tribute, Tucker hoped to honor the Natives as best as he was able, and he asked us to join him. He then bestowed our spirit names for the evening.

Katie was "Woman With Many Horses," alluding to her wealthy father, who'd helped buy the ranch. I would be "Bison Recorder," which made me smile. They'd all seen me recording ranch events every evening in my journals.

Our boys then accepted new names from Tucker and Rachel, who'd clearly spent hours researching the history of the Great Plains. My oldest son received the moniker of "Screeching Owl"; the youngest, "Deer Who Walks at Night."

Rachel, now "Woman Who Catches Many Fish," reminded us that while we weren't Natives, she hoped we nurtured life on these lands they had roamed for uncounted generations and that our daily efforts honored those who'd lived here before.

Tucker then stepped back into the shadows to retrieve a tarp-covered bundle. Repositioning himself so we could all see what he held, he carefully unwrapped a pronghorn mount and asked us to consider how we would hunt such a swift creature. With only thirty to forty pounds of meat on a buck, these frequently mislabeled antelope could sprint up to fifty-five miles per hour, or run at thirty miles per hour for twenty miles. Could we run that far, carrying spears or bows and arrows? Could our horses? No. Some horses might briefly reach fifty-five miles per hour, but if we hunted pronghorn and needed enough meat to feed many mouths, we'd have to outsmart the elegant creatures as the tribes did for so many generations. Tucker then presented the mount as a gift to the ranch.

Rachel waved us to our feet, and as Tucker rewrapped the mount, she led the way to a second nearby bonfire contained safely by a ring of large stones. The pair had also cleared away nearby grasses.

When Tucker stepped close to the firelight, he held another, larger bundle. He sat it next to his feet, well away from the heat of the flames, and waited for us to fall silent. Pointing to the ground next to the bundle with his feather-decorated stick, our boys dropped to their butts to sit cross-legged. They stared up at Tucker.

Tucker intoned all of our names, then stamped the dirt beneath his heel as he cautioned us to be fearful of the two species of *mato*, or *mukwa*, that inhabited Wyoming—though more plentifully in centuries past.

I'd read those names before. He was talking about bears.

While we'd spied and heard the screech of an occasional big cat, none of us had caught a glimpse of a black bear or its fierce cousin, the grizzly.

His description of the two species—that not all black bears are black nor are all grizzlies "grizzled"—surprised me. Grizzlies could be as small as black bears, and the color of both species included everything from black to blond.

I think we all caught our breath when Tucker unwrapped the bundle and held aloft a mato mount. Surrounded by rich brown fur, the black bear's eyes seemed to stare through us as sharp teeth glistened in the light and shadows cast by the flickering flames.

Our boys leaped to their feet to touch the fur, to run their fingertips down mato's fangs. I caught my breath a second time at the sight of those fangs next to such small fingers. The idea of facing a black bear didn't panic me, but a boar, weighing in at 400 pounds, would crush one of my sons. A grizzly? Females weighed around 700 to 800 pounds and boars up to 1,700 pounds. The Natives that hunted grizzlies must have had ineffable courage.

With an unsettling blend of excitement and reluctance, I followed Rachel, Tucker, and my family to yet a third, larger bonfire.

Sparks danced in the air at chest height, then sputtered out like drenched fireflies. By squinting slightly, I could see an even larger tarp-wrapped bundle off to the side of the fire.

The boys' eyes gleamed in the firelight as—rapt with attention—they leaned forward to listen as Tucker explained that the dance performed by many tribes, including the Sioux, Cheyenne, Pawnee, and Omaha, coincided with the annual return of immeasurable herds of tatanka, the shaggy beasts that provided food, shelter, and clothing to the Natives. Tucker's voice wavered with emotion as he clumsily demonstrated how—dressed in skins, with a rattle in one hand and a spear in the other—the hunters would take on the spirits of the animals that kept the tribes alive.

Natives used every part of tatanka: stretched and preserved hides became tents or clothing such as thick leather for moccasins, stomachs were cleaned and preserved for water bags, and hooves and horns were shaped and sharpened into tools. The boys didn't even squirm when Tucker explained that a single bison's brain was always the perfect size to be rubbed into the inner, scraped side of the animal's hide, where it acted as both a softener and preserver.

His voice cracked with sorrow when he told us how, in the late 1800s, white men slaughtered thousands and thousands—hundreds of thousands—of the beasts, harvesting tongues and skins only, leaving mountains of meat to rot. On these very lands.

Stern as a schoolmaster, Tucker shook his spear, asking the boys if they remembered how we'd had to air out the middle cabin, banishing the stink of death when we arrived a few weeks ago. Once inhaled, never forgotten, that queasy odor caused by a few dead mice we'd found in a bucket beneath the kitchen sink made the boys pinch their noses and flee. The pair of mice had dropped into the slick plastic container and couldn't get out. Tucker demanded we remember that vile rot, that we magnify the nauseating odor into a stench so pervasive that it invaded every shred of clothing, each strand of hair. As we closed our eyes, his voice fell into a whisper as he described vast pastures covered with white drifts of disintegrating bones. Not snow but bones, as far as the eye could see.

As the decimated herds and tribes of Natives struggled for survival, was the encroaching and greedy white man done? No.

Next came a feeding frenzy of bone collecting by entrepreneurial investors, satisfying a hunger for fertilizer, soap, and a way to simplify sugar refinement. Long trains rolled, boxcar after boxcar, from here to Chicago and back, in a $40 million business—what would likely be billions of dollars today.

Tucker fell silent for a long moment, but before our boys could wriggle with impatience, he stomped one booted foot into the dirt. A low chant followed, punctuated by an awkward, shuffling dance. Ungainly as a stork? A white man endeavoring, with respect, to emulate a Native? Yes, to both. The boys scrambled up to join him, and soon, all seven of us circled and stomped around the roaring fire, our homemade spears raised in tribute to Ma Nature and everything she'd provided to infinite lives and tribes and civilizations for countless millennia.

As we gained confidence, or in my case, after I cast off my embarrassment, I found my heart and feet bound together in a rhythm I'd never known before. If, as we'd been told, our land had truly held an old bison skinning camp, then a way of life died right here, beneath my feet. Many factors influenced that demise, but my heart ached for the tribes' unfathomable losses and the countless tatanka whose lives had been thrown away by greed as casually as I might throw away a used tea bag.

Near midnight, as the fire fell in on itself with a waterfall of sparks, our dance slowed. But Tucker had a final gift. That large bundle contained a magnificent bison shoulder mount, to remind us of the history of this land. The next day we mounted that majestic head above the fireplace in the newly finished cabin. I hoped tatanka's spirit would watch over our ranch.

25. THE BOYS FROM BOULDER RETURN

March meant calving season again, and even though it snowed about eight inches the previous day, the roads were clear until we turned onto Fletcher Park Road, where drifts made it slow going. At least thirty-seven deer, raising their heads from grazing through the adjacent cornfield stubble, saluted our efforts to plow the way on Fletcher Park.

Frosted with fresh snow, the log cabin looked welcoming and homey, though the approach appeared slicker than snot. Ice coated the steel bridge we'd installed—solid ten-foot-wide steel from defunct semi-trailer scales. We'd never bothered with a railing, so the gleaming, flying carpet of slick gray intimidated, barely wide enough to carry our trucks across the river.

We'd left the heat running in the cabin, albeit at a robust fifty-eight degrees, and the propane tank read five hundred gallons. We'd need to get the tank filled and have water hauled in as soon as possible.

Morning dawned with snapping white as ice creaked on the river, topped by an eye-watering blue sky. As was my habit, I headed out before breakfast to check on mommas, and before my single cup of hot tea cooled in my stomach, I found a white-faced cow braced on her back, straining to give birth against a post in the white barn.

Big momma.

Big trouble.

The calf would never drop with her on her back.

I sent the boys scrambling up to Jake's to fetch him, and together, we finally got momma turned over and up on her feet. The boys decided to call her Joe Sakic in honor of their favorite Avalanche hockey player, and I didn't discourage their humor even though Jake had to pull the calf, and neither Joe nor baby responded well. Momma had been in labor too long. Worn out and weakened, the pair of them.

I couldn't help but kick myself and wanted to kick Jake too. What time had he last walked the barns and paddock? If he didn't plan on checking them in the night, he should have asked me to set my alarm clock.

Hallie poured colostrum down the calf's throat and we lugged it over to the hot box. Three hours later the calf's breathing hadn't improved, but it hadn't worsened, either. Small blessings. My oldest son helped Hallie bottle-feed another calf, and even though Shawn's smile lit up the barn, it didn't dispel my sour mood.

With his tail tucked between his legs, Jake went out to check the herd but returned too soon, waving me into the skid steer. Following his previous trail through the fresh snow, we stopped a couple of yards from a Rorschach inkblot type image atop the snow. Guts, a right front leg, and a pathetic little tail next to the fence. A trail of blood and disturbed snow under the lower barbwire told the terrible tale.

Moaning, calling for her calf, momma stood nearby. A dirge, appropriate for my ever-worsening mood.

We'd hired Jake for his expertise. *Why the hell hadn't he done the nightly walkabouts?*

Pissed off didn't begin to describe my anger. We'd lost this calf and probably the pair in the barn. So much for Jake's prowess, his competency.

Three easy births in the next hour distracted me but did *not* shake loose my worries or mend my temper.

Instead of snow it rained the following weekend. On our way in, Shawn spotted a great horned owl on the telephone pole outside of the cabin. A magnificent bird large enough to carry off a rabbit. A sign? Good luck or bad? We'd know soon enough.

At first light I headed out to feed the cows.

Mud. Muck. More worries.

That answered that.

Nothing like starting your day with a calf in distress, drooling and with his tongue lolling out of his mouth. Cursing under my breath I jogged over to Jake's house and pounded on their door. If they weren't up yet, by God they would be soon!

Dressed but without coats, I hurried them out of the house and ran back to stand behind the calf so he wouldn't bolt as Jake and Hallie caught hold of the little guy and pulled a wad of grass and moss out of his throat. So weak he didn't put up a fuss, I probably could have managed it alone, which meant the calf had been choking for half a day, if not longer. That critter would have died of dehydration if I hadn't noticed him. Son of a . . .

I'd had enough, and things had to be said. Difficult, almost insulting things to prideful Jake, a prideful cowboy. *Not* the cowboy way.

So far this spring we've had eighty-eight calves born, roughly half and half, as far as male versus female.

Joe Sakic's calf rebounded, thank goodness, then bounded too high and broke his leg. So now he's sporting a fancy cast. Shawn wanted to sign it but I vetoed the idea. It would have scared the calf too much.

We almost ran out of water in the cabin—the current level would last about two weeks if no one took a shower. Reminded me that either Katie or I needed to create a checklist and schedule. We also needed to keep track of the cistern. Though nominally in charge of ordering feed and other items for ranch operations, after the last few weeks I now wondered if we'd need to scrutinize Jake's efforts even more carefully. That was a big 10-4.

Rain turned to snow on Sunday, though that didn't help decrease the humidity. Nor did it freeze the mud. We only fed hay to the herd as it was too wet to put out cake.

Just before leaving for Boulder, and with Jake out checking the herd, I pulled a heifer calf weighing in at eighty-five pounds. Momma and daughter both seemed okay, which cheered me ever so slightly as we loaded the truck to drive south.

With Jake seemingly communicating better, I thought branding and the first week of May would find everyone settled into a groove, but Murphy and his damnable law dropped by for a spell.

Our family drove up on Thursday with the Boys from Boulder, with Tucker and Rachel following on Friday, along with several other friends and their kids. Willing hands, all eager to work, albeit some with greener fingers than others.

First, Katie's old dog got trampled by a pissed-off momma cow. We thought for sure the dog was dead, but she whimpered, rolled over, and crept away to hide beneath a table. A couple of the old cowboys from a neighboring ranch looked her over and said she'd be sore but hadn't suffered any broken bones.

Our friend Ellen's daughter, who should *not* have been driving, ran into Stumbaugh's prized vintage pickup. Stumbaugh looked more crushed than the fender, and I felt like shit as I assured him that we'd take care of the repairs. I understood how he felt about that truck. Clearly Ellen and her giggling daughter didn't. The panels on that truck—straight and true from the factory—gleamed even in full dark. Now, every time Stumbaugh looked at the truck, he'd see that the paint didn't quite match, or the finish was too shiny, even if neither proved true.

Amateur hour continued.

The branding irons weren't hot enough. Then we had trouble with the torch, and Stumbaugh said we needed a new one. He stepped into his now limping truck, trundled home, and rolled back in his work truck, pulling a loaded horse trailer that held one of his torches. The real cowboys shouldered us out of the way, got things sorted out, and branding proceeded.

Generous soul that he was, at the end of the day Stumbaugh taught the women how to ride his horse, Coco—a true cutting horse. Eyes

20. Branding irons ready to be heated. Courtesy Bob West.

shining, Katie immediately vowed to buy new horses, ones with spirit, but not *too* spirited, so the boys could safely ride them.

Recaps of the day's conquests and other near-wrecks floated around and through the chomping of jaws and swigging of ice-cold sodas. Hoof-shaped bruises were revealed as proudly as some ornate tattoo.

As we polished off dessert, and in the same soft voice he'd used all day, Stumbaugh suggested that the Boys from Boulder join him at his ranch the next day—Sunday—for their branding. Elated, I could read my friends' proud faces. Despite the fender bender and injured dog and cold branding irons and sputtering torch, we must have done well today! Besides, it *was* the neighborly thing to do.

Early Sunday morning we piled into our ranch truck and bumped along fourteen dusty miles to our neighbor's place.

Stephen Stumbaugh, a good friend of the Harrisons, owned a similar-sized ranch south of the Devil's Washtub Ranch. He ran white Simmental, a breed of cattle I wish I could forget.

When I parked next to Steve's corral—larger than ours and pocked with rocks—I didn't see any horses. Or ropers. Or any other neighbors.

Bawling, shoving their hindquarters against the corral's corners until the split rails groaned, a mosh pit of about eighty Simmental calves bumped and bumbled around.

Steve and his wife, Marge, greeted us with vigorous handshakes, enthusiasm, and a thankful welcome. Little did we know what lay ahead.

First, Marge invited us into the ranch house, where she showed us photographs of her mother taken back near the turn of the century, when that black-clad, stern-looking woman had trapped over sixty coyotes. As a backdrop to the picture, the pelts hung like thick drapes, spread across lines tied to an old log trapper's cabin somewhere up in the mountains, west of the ranch. A tough woman. No surprise there. Virtually every rancher I'd ever met could be described as tough, though I'd also encountered the occasional teller-of-tales, adept at elaborating on facts. But for the most part, in cattle country, breeding ran true. People didn't shirk their responsibilities or run away when living got tough. They gritted their teeth and did the right thing, like we were about to do.

Steve herded us into the branding corral, suggesting we divide into teams of two, to drop the calves wherever we caught them. He'd then trot on over to do the dirty work.

Eyes wide, we Boulder Boys shared looks of horror, perhaps terror. We'd wrestled enough calves yesterday whose hind ends had been secured by the roper. No roper? We'd be wrestling and grappling, then wrestling some more.

My memories of that crushing day are dominated by the effort it took to simply survive. Kicked, bucked off the necks or hindquarters of crazed calves. Shoved sideways and backward and upside down. Skidding across rocks that soon resembled the jagged edge of the Flatirons, at least according to my shredded hide.

Once, a kick by a particularly nasty steer calf knocked my straw cowboy hat clear across the arena, and that hoof missed my forehead by no more than an inch. Did I mention the size of those Simmental calves? Bigger than our black angus, they must have weighed 250 pounds on average, and we were already tired from the previous day's festivities.

With about two-thirds of the calves branded, that smart old rancher called a time-out, literally in the nick of time. Tenderized more than the best steak I'd ever eaten, as I caught my breath I seriously considered passing out, right there, on that rocky, manure-smeared, blood-splattered dirt.

Our once new Wranglers worn through at the knees, long sleeve shirts tattered and torn—some shredded—hats askew or missing, the Boys from Boulder crawled over to an old bench built from a single massive log.

Steve and Marge's granddaughter, a miniature eight-year-old cowgirl sporting stiff blond pigtails and a gap-toothed smile, offered me a cold Coca-Cola in a bottle.

Hands shaking, I tried my best to twist off that bottle cap, but I couldn't even grip the damn thing.

That little girl watched solemnly for a long moment, then with a giggle came to my rescue. She plopped down next to me, snatched the Coke from my hands, and, with her delicate pink fingers, twisted the cap from the bottle. Guess she might have been older than I thought because she said, "You boys from Boulder surely did grow up some today."

26. THE CALF

The ugliest Sunday of spring, one I wish I could forget.

The morning's effort found me riding with Tucker, Katie, Ellen, Jake, and Hallie as we pushed our entire herd of 320 stubborn cows through a number of gates to the wetter, eastern part of the ranch. With spring branding complete, we wanted them to graze at the edge of our property where grass flourished and grew tall. Mommas would protect their calves in those high mountain plains of Wyoming as the earth continued its warming from dull brown to spring green, where prickly pear cactus and yucca also bloom.

Now you might not think it, but cows are complex creatures with scores of potential health issues. Yet for the most part, once the calves have a couple of months behind them, they can essentially be left alone with momma.

While riding JC, my trusted paint I'd brought up from Boulder, his hunter jumper heritage unexpectedly surfaced. Cows spooked him. He would keep pace with the herd but not *too* close; call me the eternal caboose.

As we entered the final pasture, a white-faced calf lagged behind his momma at the back of the herd. Rather large around the midsection, the calf bore signs of bloat. This disease is often caused by stress mixed liberally with new, green grass. With our branding only two weeks earlier and recent grazing in the lower fields, I'd spotted a calf filling with gas.

The only way to save the animal is to wrestle it to the ground and stab it in the belly with a needle—sans syringe—to let the air hiss out, akin to an inner tube going flat. A liberal application of antibiotics follows, along with prayers that the degassing wouldn't need to be repeated.

As I looped the wire over that final gatepost to close the gate, Jake trotted to the back of the herd, unlashing his rope from his saddle. A simple nudge of the knees set his horse, Tricksy, into a gallop as Jake circled a loop of rope over both their heads. A quick twist of his wrist and the calf was snared.

Jake stepped out of his saddle and slid his hand down the rope as he walked toward the calf while the rest of us dismounted. Tucker and I hurried to the calf to help hold him, but as Jake reached the calf, his horse stepped backward, tightening the rope and dragging the calf with her. This is a trained action, and Tricksy kept that rope tight.

Unfortunately Tricksy took one step too many, pulling the calf into Jake and knocking him down.

Not acceptable, not to Jake anyway. Face flushed scarlet, Jake pushed himself to his feet and stomped back to Tricksy. The sharp toe of his cowboy boot kicked into her chest made Tricksy shy away from Jake, but that smart, though visibly upset, horse knew better than to release the tension on the rope.

Jake snatched a bag of syringes from his saddlebag and trudged back to the calf as Ellen patted Tricksy's neck and spoke softly in an effort to calm the animal.

I flinched on behalf of the calf as the needle plunged into his belly; the welcome hiss of air depressurizing wheezed from the open end of the needle. One shot of antibiotics delivered to the neck, one quick look at his ear tag so we could update our records, and the calf could be released.

As she should, Tricksy continued to keep the rope tight, and when Jake stepped into the saddle, we would slip the noose out from around the calf's neck.

But when Jake reached for his saddle to mount, fearing another pointed kick, Tricksy did what any animal with half a brain would do—she shied away, calf in tow.

Shoved by the calf, Tucker and I both went flying, and I muttered a quick thank you that neither our spurs nor any bits of gloves nor clothing were caught by the rope.

Jake bellowed and stormed toward his horse. Helpless, we watched Tricksy gallop away, dragging that rag doll of a calf, bouncing it across rocks and through cacti.

I think all of us yelled as we grabbed our horses and jumped into our saddles to race behind.

In what seemed like an eternity later, though it couldn't have been more than eighty or ninety seconds, Tricksy skidded to a stop at the gate, her neck touching the upper bar. Shaking, the calf struggled to push himself to his feet. From the depths of the herd behind us, a very upset momma cow bawled and ran after us, demanding to know what in the *hell* we had done to her son.

Tricksy dragged that calf for at least a mile.

What a terrible sight.

Shining black cowhide now looked like raw shoe leather. Blood glistened and dripped from tufts of black hair.

Momma cow thundered up to her babe and licked its head and neck as if in assurance that everything would be alright.

It wasn't and wouldn't be.

My gaze darted from the calf to Jake, who'd finally caught up to us, and back again. My hands curled into fists. I wanted to beat the crap out of Jake and drag his friggin' temper—and carcass—all the way to Idaho.

I don't remember which one of us suggested riding back to the cabin to fetch a rifle. Jake objected, saying the calf might live, but pride, not truth, uttered those words. That calf needed to be put down as quickly and mercifully as possible.

Not giving in to the sick in my stomach or my anger, we rode back to the cabins in silence.

I'll never lose the memory of that helpless calf, and I am regularly reminded that in the life of a cowboy, hell, in any life, anything can go wrong in an instant. Horses and dogs aren't pets but working partners in ranching life.

Cowboys identify and treat a myriad of ailments that can strike their animals, and I don't think I could count the number of times my own inexperience might have put a cow or calf in peril. But for a born 'n' bred cowboy to behave in such a manner stunned and saddened and enraged me. I'm infamous, though, for giving people—my employees in particular—six chances to fail. The seventh? We're done.

Jake wasn't to seven . . . yet.

27. ZIP

Ranch dogs, working dogs all, come in all varieties and sizes, shapes and colors, shaggy coated and slim, smart and extra smart. Constants include their work ethic, their love of ranch life, and willingness to go wherever the ranchers go, whenever, sleet, hail, or shine. And then there's their uncanny ability to judge character. Dogs know and understand more than most folks give them credit for.

We once had a dog named Zip—a black and white miniature Aussie. Not a great ranch dog but he sure could gauge a person's character. Every time someone of truly questionable ethics came around, Zip bit them, no hesitation, no questions asked. A chronic no-gooder? Been kicking your cat, your kids, or your wife? Watch out. Zip knew. Jury, judge, and punishment, all rolled into one.

One year, after our second, long spring day at branding, Zip endeared himself to me forever.

A windy Wyoming day, one usually endured in high summer. The great crystal lens of a sky pushed us down into the dirt, sucking the air right from our lungs. Hands blistered from swimming in leather gloves all day long, shirt and jeans caked with dust, my throat remained parched despite the glasses of iced tea I kept chugging.

We cajoled and cursed and cut the calves after wrestling them to the ground, inoculating them as they moaned and shivered in protest. Those 160 pounds of writhing desperation moaned and groaned as the brand burned their hide while terror blurred their eyes.

I got kicked in the stomach early in the day. Then even harder a second time, that flailing hoof landing nearly on top of the first spot. I now sported a brand of my own—a nicely curved hoofprint that would be with me for weeks, maybe even a few months. At least they'd missed my face and other vitals—bad aim on their part!

Brian, who'd spent the previous day riding to the outer pastures with us to gather the herd, disappeared whenever a particularly large calf came through the gate. Funny how that happened. As we waited for the dinner bell, he—unlike the rest of us—didn't look at all sweaty or dirty or hollow in the middle from the day's efforts.

An urban cowboy, for sure. A legend in his own mind. He'd bragged to his California friends that we couldn't manage branding without him since he was the best rider, the best shot, and could rope a running calf four times out of five.

As the rest of us wiped sweat from our faces and switched from chugging iced tea to ice-cold beer to cut the dry, we mostly ignored him until he reached the climax of his current tall tale.

Swinging his arms wide, nearly spilling his third beer, Brian proclaimed he'd never been so sweaty or tired, and gee golly, weren't we all impressed?

I choked.

Zip, curled up at my feet while gazing solemnly at Brian's performance, stood, stretched, sauntered over to Brian, lifted his leg, and pissed. So much for that pristine black cowboy boot.

I loved that dog.

A year later I decided to teach my seven-year-old son to drive—one of the great benefits of 3,200 acres of open range to drive around on without fear of hitting any other vehicle, though a few cows could be in peril. With my son steering as he sat on my lap, I managed the brake and accelerator as we headed down the hill toward the river cabin, Zip trotting alongside the truck. That dog took an unexpected and sudden left turn, and I was late braking.

Thump, thump.

Goddammit! We'd run over our dog!

Whining but still alive, we gently loaded Zip onto the back seat, and with me driving by myself, hightailed it back to Boulder and Zip's vet. Thankfully we'd missed his belly but did break his pelvis.

Neither Zip nor my son ever forgave me for that driving lesson.

28. MIDNIGHT VISITOR

How do you describe the utter vastness of Wyoming prairie? The smell? The clarity of the air? The inability to judge distance?

The solitude.

Where you can hear the sun set.

I think of urbanites whose first glimpse of the Grand Canyon makes them weep. What would they think of our Wyoming prairie, with its boundless acres—including our own Devil's Washtub Ranch? Desolate? No. Not if you look with your heart.

My parents and our family lived in several parts of the United States—my early years back east—and while we could find open spaces to ramble through, there were also lots (and lots) of people, and roadways cluttered with cars.

Ironically, with the lowest population—about 494,000 from the 2000 census—Wyoming is the tenth largest state. There are more cattle than people by a ratio of about 2.4 cows to 1 person. You can do the rest of the math.

With 53.6 percent of the land publicly owned, other than in cities and towns, your closest neighbor will likely be several miles away.

Weather, as in extreme, is certainly a factor for Wyoming's low population, though enduring a Pittsburgh winter isn't exactly a cause for joy. Wyoming winds sweep down from the northwest, and I've regularly seen twenty-foot-high drifts. Those long, twelve-foot-high snow fences along many of the highways corral the drifts on the eastern side of the roadway so that, for the most part, highways remain passable.

A snow fence paralleled the county road on our land, and one weekend I wished it had stretched farther down the road. Heavy, wet snow, dancing to the tune of forty-mile-per-hour winds, left a fifteen-foot-high drift across the road. Two days and one skid steer later, I managed to tunnel through. Since the county road crew had already notified us that it would be a week before they could clear our road, our northern neighbors were quite appreciative.

Summer shared its own eccentricities, as pop-up thunderstorms would leap into the heights without warning. Clear blue sky as you rode out for the day? Look over your shoulder an hour later, and a grandfather beard of cranky thunderclouds might be poised to slap you upside the head with hail, lightning, and flash floods. Temperatures could plummet as much as sixty degrees.

Few folks can morph into Jeremiah Johnson, especially in mere hours, and tourists didn't grasp the risks or intensity Ma Nature doled out, regardless of the season. Got your ten essentials when leaving for a hike? Not even water? Step back into your car, please.

Winter chores sometimes exhausted us as we slogged through knee-high snow to help our ranch hand make sure the animals had access to feed, minerals, and non-frozen water. Early-to-bed was the norm after a card or board game with the boys. We'd flip cards at the dining room table, basking in the rosy glow of a fire from the woodstove. One particularly windy night, frigid temperatures overtook the earlier sunny day as snowflakes danced in the porch light.

Sound asleep by 9:30 p.m., a loud pounding at midnight startled me out of bed. Teeth bared, our dogs bounded to the living room, barking their brains out. They'd protect the family!

With the wind echoing their howls as I shoved my legs into jeans, I wondered who in the hell could be knocking on our front door in the middle of the night. Eighteen miles from town? Snowing like crazy? Our ranch hands would call if they had an emergency.

Wary, I grabbed my Winchester rifle and cracked open the door, keeping the dogs in. They growled and scrabbled to shove their noses into the cold night.

A snow-coated, battered-looking man, who reminded me of the

homeless transients panhandling around the downtown Boulder Mall, stared at me with red-rimmed eyes. Was he high? Dangerous? He shivered violently.

I demanded he tell me what he wanted.

He reached for the door to support himself and murmured, "I'm lost. Help me."

I then realized his shakes were caused by the cold, not drugs, and after leaning the rifle against the wall, I stepped out onto the porch. In a faltering voice he explained he'd been out hunting deer and elk sheds—discarded antlers that the bucks lose each year. He and several friends had been searching the nearby public lands, and when the storm hit about twelve hours earlier, he'd lost his way.

Since it seemed the man wasn't a threat to my family, I brought him into the cabin and asked Katie, who'd been standing guard as the second line of defense, to bring him a blanket.

I stoked up the stove and pulled a chair close. As water heated for tea, Katie helped him shrug out of his lightweight jacket and wrapped the blanket around his shoulders, pushing him into the chair. About ten minutes later, after gulping one mug of steaming tea and hunched over his second, he'd thawed enough to tell us his name and that he worked for a civil engineering firm in Boulder.

With melted snow dripping from his hair, I studied his face, then shook my head. I knew this man professionally but hadn't recognized him until that moment.

What were the odds?

He stuttered in gratitude, said he'd been having trouble walking and thought about giving up, finding a nice boulder next to the river and simply . . . waiting. Then he saw our porch light.

As Katie fed him hot soup, I called the sheriff. Relief evident in the dispatcher's voice, he said they would recall the well-equipped rescue teams already out searching. He also said they would let his friends know, and that a sheriff would retrieve our midnight visitor if a friend couldn't. At about 3:00 a.m., a pickup laden with a mound of deer and elk sheds pulled across the bridge.

I shook hands with the civil engineer and assured him I would see him again, in Boulder, someday.

29. SNAKE SNAPPING

My ranch hand's stepson showed up at ranch headquarters one day with a black-as-soot arm hanging limp in a sling. I'd seen a lot of bruises over the years but never anything like this. His exposed wrist and hand reminded me of a partially deflated, dull-black balloon. When I asked what had happened he replied, "Bit by a rattlesnake," before stalking away.

Shaking his head, our ranch hand explained that the Wyoming manhood tradition of "snake snapping" was unfortunately still alive and biting.

It seemed Friday night dates for teens sometimes included beer, pickup trucks, and rattlesnakes.

Rattlesnakes?

Teen stupidity, our ranch hand emphasized, strengthened by multiple beers and taunting by their peers. Find a rattlesnake, a big one, of course, chug one more beer, then grab the tail of the snake and, with a whip-like motion, crack the snake's head against a rock.

Unfortunately the snake his son tried to snap bit him in the arm, near an artery.

Fortunately one of the boy's friends remained sober enough to tie a tourniquet above the bite, or the teen might have died. As it was, the ER staff scrambled to save his arm, and it would be weeks before he would fully recover.

Having two boys of my own, thankfully not yet teens, I commiserated with the boy's father. What I didn't voice was the thought that, as a teen, I might have tried the stunt too.

I'd killed more than my share of rattlesnakes, usually by lopping their heads off with a spade. In fact I'd thought more than once that rather than a rifle scabbard on a saddle, one that held a spade would be far more useful.

Wyoming's prairie rattlesnakes, about three and a half to four feet long at maturity, sport an intricate diamond-patterned skin and the ability to slightly change color to match the seasons. Of course, they don't like us any more than we like them, and their warning buzz should never be ignored, especially since a snake can lunge the length of its body.

We'd invested in snakebite kits for each saddlebag and also kept kits in each of the cabins. Unlike humans who could lose a limb or die, horses and cows would usually survive a bite unless struck in the throat or mouth, which might cause swelling and suffocation. We also kept Benadryl on hand to dose our dogs, in hopes we could keep venom reactions to a minimum while rushing them to the animal hospital.

Sadly I'd also killed more than one bull snake by mistake. If coiled in the shadows and hissing, it was difficult to tell the difference. Since rattlesnakes' look-alike cousins were territorial and drove away smaller rattlesnakes, we wanted bull snakes slithering through the tall grass around the cabins.

Over the years I'd learned to jump away and pause to take a good look before fetching the shovel or hoe, but we nevertheless had a small drawer full of dried rattles, unhappy souvenirs of prairie rattler versus man. Sometimes though, it was a draw.

Awakened just after sunrise by a shout and a frantic knock at our bedroom door, my wife and I both sat bolt upright in bed. I wrenched open the door to my friend and fellow architect John, who'd driven up from Boulder to play cowboy for the weekend.

"I think I've been bit by a rattlesnake!" John yelped.

"What? How?" I demanded as I looked for clothes to slap on.

Despite our late night of swapping tales and beer drinking, the quiet of sunrise pulled John from his bed. He'd tiptoed to the door leading to a stone terrace and stepped out in his bare feet.

A baby rattler about six inches long objected to the early morning intrusion onto his warm stone bed and, just like Achilles, struck John in the heel. Unfortunately, young rattlers pack more punch than their parents, as they haven't yet learned how to control the amount of venom released. Mature snakes ration their venom so they can strike two or three times.

A bit frantic herself as she pushed drawer contents around, but trying to keep John calm, Katie located a snakebite kit while I looked for truck keys and boots. With the nearest hospital about thirty minutes away, we knew we needed to either use the kit or fall back on my Boy Scout skills by slicing X patterns through the two fang holes to suck the poison out.

We'd looked at the kit contents before, contemplating how to use the venom extractor, a reverse-hypodermic contraption with a clear suction cup at the end. Katie scanned the directions quickly, and I sighed with relief when Katie said we didn't need to cut an X. I didn't want to operate on one of my best friends or suck poison and his blood into my mouth unless I absolutely had to. Following Katie's instructions I centered the cup over the holes in John's heel and pulled the twin handles, creating suction. Sure enough, a dribble of milky venom splattered into the clear suction cup. The second time, we extracted a dab of pinkish fluid.

"It's still on the terrace," John said as he twisted around to watch our efforts. "The snake," he clarified. "I killed it."

"I'll get it," Katie said. "Maybe it's a bull snake."

As John shook his head Katie trotted into the kitchen to grab a plastic bag.

Directing John to stay calm and walk slowly to the front porch, I told him to wait there while I got the truck. Katie bolted from the back of the cabin to thrust the snake-in-a-bag at John.

"I'll let the hospital know you're on your way," she yelled from over her shoulder as she jogged back into the cabin.

I nodded, ran to my truck, and raised dust as I skidded the truck up to the walkway.

Off we raced to the Wheatland Hospital.

Snapping my eyes every few seconds from the road to John gave me a headache. Even though I was speeding, I had to watch him. If he started acting confused or lightheaded, or if a black line crawled up the vein in his leg, I'd push the truck into triple digits.

A gurney waited at the emergency entrance, with a young and attractive blond nurse attending.

John's mood changed from dour to interested.

The nurse asked if she could see the snake to make sure it was a rattler. John presented the beast, all six inches of it, with the tiniest of diamond patterns decorating its now limp back. The nurse smiled and choked back a laugh while explaining that they regularly treated snakebite victims and that this might be the record for the smallest rattler ever. It didn't even have a fully formed button.

Her tone shifted back to professional as she explained one dose of anti-venom cost several thousand dollars and that John's insurance might not fully cover it. Also that the anti-venom sometimes caused negative reactions. She pulled a black marker out of her pocket and drew a line on John's ankle about five inches above the dark line creeping up his leg from the puncture wounds. She then suggested we relax, go out to breakfast, and come back an hour later. If the dark line had traveled above the marker line, she wanted to dose him with the anti-venom.

So off we went to the Wheatland Inn for pancakes and dissipation of nerves. Our conversation first centered on how many inches that snake would have grown to by the time we got back to Boulder. Three feet long? Five?

Then John wanted to know whether the nurse had been wearing a wedding ring.

Upon our leisurely return to the hospital, I went to find a pay phone so I could call the ranch with an update while John sought out the lovely nurse.

I met him near the exit, and he said he'd been given some Tylenol and that the nurse thought our immediate use of the snakebite kit must have pulled out most of the venom since the dark line had stopped growing.

As we settled into the truck for the drive back to the ranch, John looked as smug as the Cheshire Cat. He twisted his leg so I could see his heel. A phone number now graced his skin above the marker line.

30. THE BOY SCOUT CAMP

Even though I can and have worked by myself for long periods of time, I enjoy being with people and I like to entertain, to make certain every-one is having a great time. Especially when it comes to something I'm enthusiastic about, such as our ranch. One perfect summer weekend my wife's brother and father flew in from California. They'd visited before, of course, first as they considered whether to invest in the property, then later to enjoy family and our western ways.

I suggested we ride to the Boy Scout Camp, which I had visited once before. I remembered my previous peaceful amble through the ponderosa pine foothills owned by the True Ranch, our western prop-erty line neighbors, and also wanted to share what I'd learned about the camp.

Always busy, the True family and their ranch hands had little contact with us, though they'd waved hello and we'd enjoyed a rare, albeit brief, chat. Their family started ranching in Wyoming in 1957 with thirty-two cows and one bull. I'd been told by other locals that a person could now ride from Cheyenne to Casper on True Land and Cattle Company ranches without stepping off of their property.

Our ride through their ponderosa forest would make us trespassers, sort of, but there was a prescriptive easement across the Trues' Ranch to access the camp.

After ranch chores and a hurried breakfast, clear Rocky Mountain blue skies beckoned, enhanced by a hint of chill in the air. It took over an hour to brush, check and clean hooves, then saddle and tack up six horses for the trip. In truth I could have done it by myself in less time, but my brother-in-law wannabe cowboy kept getting in my way. How could I nudge him aside, though, since his enthusiasm spilled over more than a water trough at the base of a spinning windmill?

Our early start faded into midmorning when we finally rode away.

I respected my father-in-law. I thought I'd earned his respect, that he recognized a similar work ethic and commitment to family. So, of course, that morning I inadvertently thrust the leather chin strap along with the steel bit into Tiny's mouth, the mount we'd selected for Walter. Why this horse? Out of the six we'd groomed and saddled, we thought Tiny would be the best choice for Katie's father. He'd ridden before but wasn't necessarily proficient like the rest of us. Tiny, while quite a large mustang, once wild but carefully broken, had proved himself to be one of our most trusty mounts. But with his mouth stuffed full, Tiny tossed his head, balked, and hunched up, ready to buck when Walter pulled on the reins.

We stopped. I stepped down from my saddle, but my brother-in-law, the great fixer of all problems, beat me to his father's side and quickly diagnosed the problem. Brian unbuckled Tiny's bridle and, after soothing the upset mustang, tacked him up again.

Despite the bright sunlight, my peaceful ride turned cold as my father-in-law and brother-in-law glared at me. My wife threw in a few jabs as well. Of course none of that hurt as much as my own self-flagellation.

I spurred my horse to lead the way as we traveled past the barbwire gate at the west boundary of our property. Towering, troll-like granite formations and ponderosa pines soon surrounded us. Though I didn't voice my concerns, I studied each granite monolith carefully, looking along the edges for ear tufts and gleaming mountain lion eyes—this type of landscape belonged to them as much as the Trues. I'd blown it with Tiny's bridle and wanted the remainder of our ride to be perfect.

The simple cadence of the horses' steady pace lulled us, as did the spectacular and unfamiliar surroundings.

At roughly the four-and-a-half-mile mark, we paused to dismount and stretch.

We all fell silent.

Behind us dour gray thunderheads boiled over the Medicine Bow Range.

My father-in-law and brother-in-law wanted to hightail it back to the ranch, but I knew we couldn't outrun the storm. I said we needed to get to the Boy Scout Camp as soon as we could—that it would be faster and safer, especially with the experience level of our riders.

Lightning spiked behind us as thunder growled.

While I wanted to gallop, I didn't think our cowboy wannabees could handle that, so I led our group in a controlled canter.

We lost the race.

About a half mile from the camp.

Booming thunder surrounded us as hail and rain scrubbed the sky, then pounded us. Jagged fissures of lightning cracked, too close, as the temperature plummeted. We'd heard that bit of cowboy wisdom—thunder does all the barking but it's the lightning that bites—and it seemed our spooked horses had too, as they broke from their smooth three-beat canters into full gallop. Surrounded by sheer granite cliffs, we followed the sweeping bend of the North Fork of the Laramie River. Luckily we were so close to the old stone lodge that no one lost control of their wild-eyed mounts.

With each clap of thunder shadowed by half-rearing horses, I shouted for everyone to hold tight to their reins as we leaped from our saddles. Somehow we all made it through the thick wooden doorway, so big that we led the horses on in.

Built in the 1940s on land donated to the Boy Scouts of America, timber trusses hand-hewn from nearby trees vaulted overhead, supporting a newer metal roof. Stone walls crafted from local granite emphasized the height and depth of the stone fireplace. I could stand upright in it,

21. The Boy Scout Lodge. Courtesy Bob West.

possibly with my horse. Granite also lay beneath our feet, where flat stones fit together in a completed jigsaw puzzle.

Pushed against one wall, rusted steel bunk beds still sported their wire springs, tilted upright alongside long benches. I could almost envision a troop of wide-eyed Boy Scouts, perhaps away from home for the first time, gathering and chattering where we now stood. What an adventure that would have been, especially for city boys.

Though we'd scattered when first entering the lodge, we edged close near the center of the great room as waves of hail beating the metal roof prohibited conversation. I had planned on sharing the history of the site when used by the Boy Scouts, and that it was rumored to have been used for a Hollywood Western sometime in the 1950s, but with everyone wet and shivering, I remained silent. The temperature in the lodge couldn't be more than fifty degrees, and I doubted it was even that warm outside.

No firewood, no rain slickers, and no changes of clothes. Instead of laughing about our adventure, frowns faced me as moods soured once again.

What would the Boy Scouts have done? I believe they would have tried to look at the bright side while helping others and showing loyalty to their family.

I'm not sure which one of us suggested it, but Brian and I decided to ride back to the ranch to collect dry clothing, then return as soon as we could. We were the best riders on the best horses. The storm still pulsed, but we felt confident.

What a ride.

At full gallop on my paint horse, JC never hesitated in showing off his hunter jumper skills, leaping small ditches and fallen branches without breaking stride. At about our four-mile mark, Brian pulled his horse alongside and, looking uncomfortable, yelled, "I've got to pee!"

I'd been ignoring that urge for the last mile, and I yelled back, "Thank goodness, me too!"

Unlike in the Hollywood Westerns, at a long full gallop, that saddle horn exerts pressure on the prostate. The wet jeans didn't help.

We reined to a stop and did our business while laughing about John Wayne never needing to dismount on those long chases across the plains.

Once home we put on warm jackets, bundled together enough for everyone else, and loped back to the camp so as not to overtax our horses. We found our "survivors" outside the lodge, sunning themselves. Steam rose from the horses' hides as everyone claimed a jacket, and we rode home.

Much later I mused on the points of Boy Scout Law and wondered if I should mention to everyone how similar they are to Gene Autry's Cowboy Code.

I didn't.

Though I'd basically enjoyed our adventure, based on the vinegary looks I received when I brought it up, not everyone shared my outlook.

The Scout Law has 12 points. Each is a goal for every Scout. A Scout tries to live up to the Law every day. It is not always easy to do, but a Scout always tries.

A Scout is:

>   Trustworthy. Tell the truth and keep promises. People can depend on you.
>
>   Loyal. Show that you care about your family, friends, Scout leaders, school, and country.
>
>   Helpful. Volunteer to help others without expecting a reward.
>
>   Friendly. Be a friend to everyone, even people who are very different from you.
>
>   Courteous. Be polite to everyone and always use good manners.
>
>   Kind. Treat others as you want to be treated. Never harm or kill any living thing without good reason.
>
>   Obedient. Follow the rules of your family, school, and pack. Obey the laws of your community and country.
>
>   Cheerful. Look for the bright side of life. Cheerfully do tasks that come your way. Try to help others be happy.
>
>   Thrifty. Work to pay your own way. Try not to be wasteful. Use time, food, supplies, and natural resources wisely.
>
>   Brave. Face difficult situations even when you feel afraid. Do what you think is right despite what others might be doing or saying.
>
>   Clean. Keep your body and mind fit. Help keep your home and community clean.
>
>   Reverent. Be reverent toward God. Be faithful in your religious duties. Respect the beliefs of others.

Gene Autry's Cowboy Code:

1. The Cowboy must never shoot first, hit a smaller man, or take unfair advantage.

2. He must never go back on his word, or a trust confided in him.

3. He must always tell the truth.

4. He must be gentle with children, the elderly, and animals.
5. He must not advocate or possess racially or religiously intolerant ideas.
6. He must help people in distress.
7. He must be a good worker.
8. He must keep himself clean in thought, speech, action, and personal habits.
9. He must respect women, parents, and his nation's laws.
10. The Cowboy is a patriot.

31. NUMBER 72

Came up Friday night in the rain and almost ran into a calf—number 72—that had already been hit by a car or truck. Jake didn't confess to first hitting the critter, and I didn't ask. Not sure who else would have been on our road, though. Guess we need to speed our effort to breed white faces into our herd so we can see them at night.

Number 72 is still on his feet, despite a broken hip. His momma shows up every night to give him milk and stays by him all night. After his morning breakfast, she heads off to graze.

We installed a few signs along the road, warning of livestock. Surely would like to know who hit that calf, Jake.

32. TEPEE RINGS AND TOOLS OF FLINT

One of the joys of owning a large ranch in Wyoming is the unspoiled raw beauty of the place, a sense that virtually everything around you remains unaffected by the years, whether 60 or 130. Unlike most places on earth, this land is literally untouched.

If I squinted my eyes I could very nearly see and hear and *feel* the earthquake-like movement of thirty million buffalo thundering across the Great Plains, with Native tribes such as the Oglala Sioux, Blackfoot, and Cheyenne tracking the wide swath of hoofprints as they planned a fruitful hunt.

I could study the ground and find a perfect flint arrowhead—one that had been knapped in the correct size and shape for that buffalo hunt. If broken, the arrowhead might once have been attached to a shaft embedded in a buffalo carcass and was left to settle on the grassy plains, waiting to be discovered and revered a century or more later. This was a playground for a western history aficionado, especially those that felt they'd been born a century or two too late.

Excitement and reverence, an unusual blend of emotions I'd rarely experienced before buying the ranch, but after, that combination of sentiment frequently shrouded my efforts, such that I yearned to stretch our Wyoming weekends into weeks, months into years.

My connection to that sometimes-abrasive landscape flourished as I tried to honor its history while simultaneously bending it to my will. We *would* have a successful cattle operation. We *would* rebuild what had been broken. Yet we—I—could not mend all that had gone before. The discarded detritus of what Glenn claimed were the Sioux and other tribes often reminded me of my arrogance.

Arrowhead tips. Palm-sized grinding stones. Tepee rings of larger stones.

When out hiking or picking rocks with the family, our young boys whooped and danced circles around us when we examined their finds. While our collection never matched Glenn's, our small basket of flint and smooth grinding stones grew to a larger basket, then two. Finally three. When Glenn told us where to find the remaining tepee rings and that he'd gathered the rocks of others, my heart felt as heavy as those skull-sized stones used to hold down the bottom edge of the cured hides. Though grateful he'd left the rings near the Devil's Washtub intact, how I wished he'd honored the legacy of the tribes by preserving *all* of the rings. Then my boys and others could squint their eyes against the wind and imagine the smell of smoke and grilling buffalo curling in their nostrils, the taste of dust stirred by wrestling children and barking dogs as dozens of Natives worked beside the fires between the tepees erected by the encampment.

The wind would have blown then as it did today, and the brilliant blue umbrella of sky would have been thoroughly studied centuries ago, as Natives sought signs of weather that pointed to the passage of months and seasons, influencing their decisions on when to fill their water bags, roll the tepees around their poles, and guide their laden horses to the next site, probably used regularly over the centuries.

In the quiet evenings after the boys went to bed, I found myself mesmerized by those broken pieces of stone, rubbing the shattered and sometimes still-sharp bits of soapy flint between my fingers as I pondered what I'd read about the Sioux being forcefully moved from the area around 1880; the trek westward by settlers seeking new lives collided with the nomadic life of the tribes as they lived so lightly upon the land.

Not many places still exist where decades of treasure hunters haven't ruined, whether by greed, disrespect, or accident, the traces of those long-ago encampments. Ma Nature's constant landscaping by floods and soil erosion contributed to the loss. In truth the Devil's Washtub Native site had barely been touched by Ma Nature, and only one or two generations of homesteaders, followed by Glenn's family, then us, occupied the property since the last Native American called the valley home.

Home.

Here I sat, in a cozy log cabin I built, nestled alongside the tumbling river, visualizing why our ranch offered perfect topography for a sizeable Native encampment. The mouth of the canyon below the mountains provides a lush green meadow with nearby water. Rock cliff bluffs on each side of the meadow must have sheltered the tepees, with the bluffs offering perfect views over the valley for lookouts to warn the tribe if unwanted visitors approached. A journal entry by Francis Parkman on August 1, 1846, confirmed my theory:

> Fairly among the mts. Rich, grassy valley—plenty of gooseberries and currants—dark pine mts.—an opening dell that tempted me to ride up into it, and here in the cool pine woods I recalled old feelings, and old and well remembered poetry. Climbed a steep hill—on the left the mts. and the black pine forests—far down, the bare hills, and threading the valley below came the long, straggling procession of Inds.
>
> They soon camped in a grassy nook, where crowded together—dogs and horses, men, women, and children—the sight was most picturesque. The men sat smoking—the women worked at the lodges—the children and young men climbed the steep rocks, or straggled among the pine-covered hills around the place. Droves of horses were driven to water—girls with spoons and buffalo paunches went down to a deep dell for water. Heat intense—sat on a shady rock and watched the scene. Climbed at sunset a high hill and looked over the mts. and pine forests. All night, the Inds. were playing a great gambling game. (Parkman, *The Journals of Francis Parkman*, 466)

Historically a very large camp, hundreds of tepee rings had been unceremoniously plowed under by Glenn and his father as they changed the use of the land; the Harrison family needed hay production from the meadows to feed their cattle. Not everything had been plowed, though, as on the higher, more arid plateaus, twenty or so rock rings, silently remaining historically relevant, poked defiantly through the prairie grass. Here, as we were told this was a buffalo skinning camp, we found abandoned stone tools that showed us where the beasts had been butchered. Here too, Glenn told us he'd found dozens of piles of rocks slightly larger than a human body. Not graves, per se, but he believed these identified the locations of burial scaffolds. The Plains tribes built platforms roughly eight feet high to hold the leather-wrapped bodies of their loved ones, but we found no remnants of those structures.

We discovered everything from hand-sized scrapers and knives for skinning—buffalo hides were thick, and the sharp-edged tools had dulled after repeated use—to the smallest thumb scrapers for intricate work, all artfully knapped, to knives and other cutting tools with interesting shapes and notches for attaching wooden handles. Chips of flint abounded near large, flat-topped granite boulders. Leftovers from the knapping process when a larger stone would be split into smaller pieces and then meticulously shaped, the chips had to have been left by Natives who probably claimed those warm boulders for their work areas. What we didn't find many of were grinding stones for grains or remnants of stone bowls.

Similar stone tools found hundreds of miles from our ranch are displayed in museums in Cody and other cities. Many years later I realized what a historic prize the Devil's Washtub Ranch might have been had generations of ranchers not been focused on hay production. Yet I cannot fault any of them. Raising beef in the arid clime of Wyoming is brutal work, and every rancher I've known respects their land and often knows every square foot of it. The use of our land had changed over the generations, and I honored all who'd fed their children there.

One of my first memories as a new intern, or apprentice, at an architectural firm in Boulder was drafting documents by hand for the historical renovation of the Old Soldiers' Barracks and Officers' Quarters of the

Ninth Cavalry that served in the Indian Wars in the mid-1800s. At that time I didn't think much of the project, envisioning a dusty, slumping building surrounded by dusty seas of tall grass. I had barely heard of Fort Laramie and had never seen it. At my then ripe old age of twenty-three and recently graduated from college, dating and partying occupied my weekends, not this National Park Service project. I don't remember much about that specific set of drawings other than expressing concern that I didn't have thorough, as-built dimensions of the structures or the site and that the numbers didn't add up.

In the summer of 2000 the West family traveled to Cheyenne, Wyoming, for our annual family reunion. My cousin Barb planned a side trip up to Fort Laramie, about fifty miles east of the ranch. She thought our entire posse, adults and children alike, would find the trip interesting since we'd had a relative stationed at the fort during the 1870s, after the Civil War.

I'd been researching the Native culture as it related to the ranch, particularly their customs and use of the stone tools that we discovered. I hoped to better understand the layout of their tepee rings and other factors that influenced the Natives who'd once inhabited this region of Wyoming.

My immediate family had already traveled to Sheridan, Cody, and the battleground of the Little Big Horn, and I'd read several books about Fort Laramie and other forts. I had a basic understanding of the forts' central role in the management of this territory, particularly related to the "Indian problem," which consisted of an ever-expanding homesteading population navigating west, thereby creating enormous pressures on Native hunting grounds and their culture, precipitating the inevitable fights for land and power.

Our family reunion trip to Fort Laramie revealed an interesting historical connection to our ranch, reinforcing the spiritual attachment I felt to the land.

Subsequent to his service for the Union during the Civil War, my great-great-grandfather served at Fort Laramie.

Commissioned as a captain on August 5, 1861, by President Abraham Lincoln to fight for the Union Army in the Civil War, John Rziha, an accomplished civil engineer formerly known as Baron Johann Antonia Laube de Laubenfels Jr., immigrated from Austria. Concerned that his heritage might affect his career, Johann changed his name upon arrival at Ellis Island. Involved in the design and mapping of forts in the Civil War, including Fort Henry and Fort Donaldson, and several in the western United States from New Mexico to Wyoming, Captain Rziha could also fight. Wounded twice near Lookout Mountain and Missionary Ridge in the Civil War, in 1867 he fought for General Hancock in Kansas against the Cheyennes. He commanded the infantry and heavy guns while George Armstrong Custer commanded the cavalry and Wild Bill Hickock scouted. Rziha's assignment as a colonel at Fort Laramie began in 1874 and included short stints as commander.

Discovery of that connection to our family created a sensation, and the Fort Laramie historian offered to track down and allow us to view several historical documents that were either signed by our ancestor or mentioned his actions.

The historian also offered our family a back-of-the-house tour of the barracks, including the camp library located on the second floor of the historic structure. As we climbed the stairs she waved ahead, noting we should all "watch out for the last step." After we'd gathered at the top she said, "When we last renovated, the prefabricated stair was an inch short."

My heart sank.

Back in 1980 I detailed the drawings for that very stair, and I remembered struggling with the as-built dimensions. I could have driven up to the fort one weekend to verify the dimensions. Instead my omission, and what I now view as my youthful lack of dedication, caused decades of stubbed toes for visitors and museum workers alike. I confessed and we all laughed, but the shadow of that multitude of "ouches" dampened my amusement.

What interested me more than bruised toes and my own bruised ego, though, was the opportunity to contemplate the amazing first coincidence of that day: discovery that my great-great-grandfather served at Fort Laramie when Custer and his Seventh Cavalry rode through in 1875 while beginning the campaign that led to his fateful demise at Little Big Horn.

I have often wondered whether Rziha and Custer discussed strategy, specifically the need for cannon or Gatling guns to accompany the Seventh Cavalry's march to the Black Hills since that would have been my great-great-grandfather's expertise as commander of the infantry. Custer and his men paid for his fear of being slowed by hauling such heavy equipment. After the massacre, through the remainder of the Indian Wars, the cavalry traveled with heavy cannons.

In books such as Remi Nadeau's *Fort Laramie and the Sioux Indians* and Paul Hedron's *Fort Laramie and the Great Sioux War*, I read that soldiers from the fort often took expeditions to the Black Hills to cut lumber and hunt. I always assumed the authors meant the Black Hills in South Dakota, but as we studied a historic map of Fort Laramie and the surrounding region in their archives, I learned otherwise.

In clear symbols and text, the map portrayed the Black Hills in what would become Wyoming, specifically, a location due west of the ranch— *our* ranch—the Devil's Washtub Ranch.

I believe my great-great-grandfather once sat in stillness atop his horse to look over the same valley of the North Laramie River that I loved, in the "Black Hills" of our ranch. He'd preceded me. Some days out of the corner of my eye, I could glimpse him riding alongside, could smell his sweat-dampened uniform and hear the jingle of his horse's tack.

With our abundance of left-brain-dominated business people, my architectural career was unexpected in my family that includes accountants, engineers, insurance salesmen, and other analytical professions. Since discovering Captain John Rziha, I have studied his incredibly detailed topographic maps, such as those of the town of Paducah, Kentucky, the forts of the Civil War, and western frontier forts, and I believe his spirit and bloodline directed my journey to the Devil's Washtub Ranch. He rides there, still.

TEPEE RINGS AND TOOLS OF FLINT

33. BOOBS!

Time machines do exist. Sort of. Or rather, time highways. The drive from our home in Boulder County to our Wyoming ranch supported that theory.

Three and a half hours on the road began with the serene, rural greenways of Boulder County open space, but all too soon we merged our truck and horse trailer onto the northbound interstate. There we competed for lane space with new-gen Coloradoans whose aggressive driving habits, likely imported from California and New York, didn't blend well with towing a livestock-laden trailer. Every habit, from allowing for stopping distance to signaling for a lane change, seemed to be a foreign concept. Ninety miles an hour? Tailgating? Whattaya mean that's a party in a parking lot? Car wars at its worst.

Traffic density eased and tension leaked away once we made it through Fort Collins, as the physical landscape also changed. A few out-of-place intrusions of small suburban housing plats populated by cheap, cloned homes with tiny yards faded into greenish-brown prairie. As Colorado- and Wyoming-plated vehicles continued north, a few cattle and an occasional antelope grew into small herds.

Not quite in two-part harmony, my boys moaned when I tuned in to the country western station on the radio as the transition to my "other" life took control of the steering wheel.

We typically drove north on Friday afternoon and south on Sunday night, so to relieve their boredom we played games such as counting cows, horses, hawks, and eagles, with escalating points depending on rarity and first sightings.

One sunny afternoon drive coincided with the mass motorcycle rally in Sturgis, South Dakota, and we were passed by a parade of Hells Angels in two-by-two formation as they growled north.

As the sixth or seventh pair rode by, I glanced at my young and innocent boys who were, much to my consternation, waving at the cavalcade!

The Harleys kept coming and coming. Unshaven men wearing sunglasses—though no helmets, or sleeves, for that matter—in their denims or leathers and thick-soled boots, many with clinging leather-clad women ensconced proudly on the "bitch seat." The clamor of the big bikes pummeled us with their straight potato-potato exhausts.

As the final two motorcycles swept past, they slowed from sixty-five or seventy miles per hour to about fifty-five miles per hour. Braking, and concerned about a confrontation, I watched the two women passengers twist around and raise their shirts to display their proud, and rather large, boobs. Laughing, each woman waved and blew kisses as the bikes accelerated and roared away.

Now draped over the back of the front seat of the truck, my boys strained for one final glimpse of the boobs.

34. DEVELOPERS

It is virtually impossible to succeed in the architectural profession without working for developers, especially in the commercial and production housing sectors. It is also virtually impossible that an architectural firm won't be "snake-bit" by certain unscrupulous developers.

Architects are not banks. Nor are the engineering consultants contracted to team on projects. Yet certain developers will at least stretch—if not break—their contract clauses.

When a developer envisions a need for housing, retail, or commercial space within a community, they often purchase raw land or decrepit property that needs redevelopment. Their vision includes an amazing sales job to their banks or investors, municipalities, and design and construction teams. As the project progresses, the less-than-desirable developer will often delay payment of bills. On a large project this might include a team of architects and consultants, plus the contractor, all of whom have to continue to meet their own payroll, yet find themselves carrying hundreds of thousands of dollars—sometimes millions—of accounts receivable.

With that said, I also worked with many terrific developers, designing new office and manufacturing facilities for companies such as Celestial Seasonings, Quantum, Ohmeda, Spacemark, and CableLabs. Those companies' explosive growth sometimes necessitated equally swift design and construction of flexible space. That couldn't happen without a solid developer-architect-contractor team. Our firm also designed many multifamily housing projects, specializing in resort and urban infill mixed-use. Sadly these multifamily projects evolved into an inherently risky project type.

There are a multitude of "specialty" developers whose focus and experience might also include industrial, retail, and government facilities. In Wyoming I also encountered "land" developers that reminded me of advertisements I'd seen in my youth, offering "Twenty Acres in the West" for a pittance.

Of course, there was a catch. Or three.

An unsuspecting homesteader wannabe might purchase a parcel, unseen, for $20,000, based on a slick brochure featuring the snow-capped Rocky Mountains as a backdrop for a fertile green valley. The parcel they purchased, though, would be off-screen. Thirty or forty acres of sagebrush desert, pockmarked with weather-ravaged street signs identifying a bizarre gridwork of partially scraped-out roadways. Yes, the Rockies might tower in the distance, but these parcels had no water or any type of infrastructure for power and sewage. Sometimes there wasn't even access without trespassing.

My conscience and I wrestled many a time during my architectural career because of my desire to preserve and protect parts of the "old West" for future generations. Sadly, before I could afford to be picky, I designed a number of projects that encroached upon undeveloped areas.

In Wyoming, a 3,200-acre multi-generationally owned ranch directly abutted the northern fence line of our property. That northern ranch somewhat mirrored the Devil's Washtub Ranch, both sporting beautiful rolling terrain with stands of ponderosa pines and granite outcroppings and abundant grass pastures with water—in their case, small springs dotted the property.

A working cattle ranch, few improvements were made on their property. One day we woke up to the shocking news that their property had gone under contract to a Montana land developer who paid a million dollars for those pristine acres.

Shit.

Subdivided into forty-acre sites, the developer marketed each site for $40,000. A maze of roadways soon sliced the property into a poorly planned "ranchette community." Little or no respect had been paid to views or topography. That, and the insipid street signs, made me want to beat my head against a fencepost.

Those eighty lots sold faster than candy bars in a Choke 'n' Puke, and the uneducated buyers, used to purchasing tract homes, didn't understand that a new eighteen-mile line for electricity would need to be run to the site from Wheatland, with the cost allocated between the parcels. What about water? Only those lucky few buyers of parcels with springs on them wouldn't need to bury cisterns and truck in water.

Unfortunately what often happens to these types of subdivision developments is that buyers begin to build their dream home or cabin, then run out of money. What's left is a partially built, decaying eyesore, complemented by the dilapidated trailer they towed in to live in during construction.

Some intrepid buyers might complete their home, but a single formidable Wyoming winter inevitably sent them hightailing back to "civilization." Imagine the shock when they realized simple services we take for granted, such as municipal plows to clear the roads, did not exist. Toss in the inability to run to the grocery store any time, night or day, and their dreams tumbled away.

Then there were the out-of-state hunters, with no intention of building, driving their RV up from Texas to squat on their parcel during hunting season. Decimating the local deer herd? Yep. Don't worry, neighbors, whether an errant bullet might hole your living room.

Needless to say, we persuaded our ranch partners to purchase two of the overpriced forty-acre parcels immediately adjacent to our land as a buffer from this unfortunate development. We hoped that would dissuade potential trespassers from sneaking onto our land to fish, or simply keep mischief-makers away, as that area was beyond the view of our daily routines.

That development galvanized me. I vowed that every future architectural project I considered designing would be partially analyzed by its impact on maintaining the "old West."

35. CHANGE

Change is inevitable, and despite our patience and best efforts, the business of the Devil's Washtub Ranch proved to be no exception.

How many chances do you give an employee? How many years do you wait to see if they'll improve? I believe in loyalty, and I've been told more than once that I hold onto staff too long, forgive too much while mentoring as much as I'm able. Sometimes, okay often, even finishing half-completed efforts that I'd delegated but were left incomplete.

The enthusiasm and energy first displayed by our ranch hands, Jake and Hallie, had waned after their first few years occupying ranch headquarters. Their attention to detail lagged, then that final straw fell with a thud and, woefully, too much blood.

Jake regularly ignored some of our horses, specifically those that didn't perform daily ranch tasks. Often left out in a far pasture to fend for themselves, our family's riding horses had no close-in barn or shed to shelter in, though Jake's horses did.

Too far from the ranch headquarters to be heard, my favorite riding horse, JC, lost a battle with a mountain lion, and neither Jake nor Hallie heard the horse's screams. After the lion clawed JC's rear flank, terror consumed that poor addled beast. He bolted and, in full darkness, ran through a barbwire fence, slicing the hide and flesh off his right front leg, revealing tendons and blood-stained bone.

In shock JC suffered alone through the remainder of that long night until Jake found him the next morning.

The local Wheatland vet told us JC should be put down. I drove up, and an old cowboy saying—"God heals and the doctor takes the fee"—guided me. I looked that horse in the eye and let him decide. In a moment I had my answer.

"Whatever it takes," I told the vet. Thousands of dollars later, and after months of rehabilitation, I again saddled JC for a ride. A fine ride.

Not too long after, my uncle volunteered to "ranch sit" so that Jake and Hallie could take a few days off. My uncle called me once or twice a day to report in, and one morning he sounded slightly groggy and upset. Apparently he'd been awakened at about two in the morning when an RV rumbled past the cabin he slept in. By the time he'd dressed, tracked down one of our high-power flashlights, and started trotting across the field toward headquarters, only the taillights of the RV were visible as it headed back out the way it came.

After hearing of the rare night visit, and where my uncle thought the RV had stopped, we decided to audit the ranch gas tank usage.

Their vacation over, when we asked Jake and Hallie why usage over the last few months had increased by hundreds of gallons of gas, they reluctantly confessed that Hallie's daughter and her daughter's boyfriend had been regularly filling their RV from our tank.

Free isn't always free, and we'd forgiven them once too often. We fired Jake and Hallie.

It didn't take long for Katie to find new ranch hands, Peter and Donna, who lived on a family ranch in Leadville, Colorado. A week or so after they took over, we realized what an asset we'd been lacking. Competent and professional, soon the day-to-day management decisions transitioned to their capable care. And I do mean care. They cared about the land, the equipment, and most importantly, our animals, the herd, and how to improve every bit of it.

When Peter suggested we could increase our revenue by introducing high-altitude Hereford bulls to our black angus herd, he backed the suggestion with facts and figures. In a few generations, his ideas proved their worth. The white-faced cows we'd long desired, called baldies, increased the average weaning weight of our calves by twenty-three pounds. Not a small percentage, and it felt fine increasing Peter's salary as he increased our bottom line. Loyalty works both ways.

36. ROAD TRIP

Armed with our *Rand McNally Road Atlas*, sunglasses, cold drinks, and a book called *Wyoming Historical Markers at 55mph* by Susan Carlson, Katie, Tucker, Rachel, and I loaded the truck to drive north from the ranch. Even the names of our destination goals evoked the history of the wild, wild West. Native American Medicine Wheel, Wild Horses, Custer's Last Stand—and we'd even discussed tapping our toes at some country western venues along the way. Yeehaw!

Many easterners don't appreciate the scope of road trips in the western states, where you drive hundreds of miles to connect the dots of points of interest. The barren, in-between stretches of prairie will lull you to sleep, even with pit stops in Douglas, Casper, Sheridan, Buffalo, and my favorite small Wyoming town, Meeteetse—population 429.

On the road trip we'd planned, the *Wyoming Historical Markers at 55mph* would prove invaluable. Filled with entertaining trivia, without the book's guidance we would have sped by the tiny town of Kaycee, which hosted a couple of surprises. Turns out this little town, with its great cowboy bar where country music singer/songwriter Chris LeDoux often performed and a gas station home to more pro-rodeo cowboys than almost any other venue, isn't far from the Hole-in-the-Wall. Butch Cassidy and the Sundance Kid, along with the nine-member Wild Bunch gang, met at a small cabin in the always-guarded box canyon, so they probably rode through Kaycee many times.

As we stood in the box canyon, I couldn't help but imagine one aspect of the lives of those cowboys that's been overlooked in the movies: their stench.

I've spent full days on horseback, sweating beneath the sun's unwinking eye, my horse's coat sometimes wet with lather. Back at the ranch at the end of the day, I'd feed and water my horse and brush him down before enjoying my own hot shower with lots of soap.

Picture riding for days or weeks on end. *Maybe* washing your hands and face. Wearing the same woolen or cotton shirt and leathers. Today the odor would flatten us. In the 1880s, except possibly in town, riders would have worn their stiff-with-sweat clothes for weeks on end.

I've forgiven the early television and movies for depicting crisp, clean shirts and pants, along with silky kerchiefs wrapped around a cowboy's neck. Recent efforts are better but still lack the true grit I believe men and women endured.

As we climbed back into our air-conditioned truck, I didn't sniff my armpits, but it did cross my mind.

Next stop: Buffalo, then Sheridan.

With its sharpshooter western history, we stopped in Sheridan to learn more about bigger-than-life characters such as Buffalo Bill Cody and Calamity Jane. We visited the famous King's Saddlery/King Ropes, The Mint Bar for more than one beer, and finally headed out to the Medicine Wheel National Historic Landmark. South of the Crowe Reservation in Montana and over ten thousand years old, the eighty-foot-diameter limestone wheel was laid out by Natives. With its twenty-eight spokes related to the twenty-eight-day lunar cycle and seven stone circles or cairns, the wheel exudes a tangible and enigmatic spiritual force. Visitors speak softly after enjoying the well-designed and purposeful mile and a half trek from the parking lot. Boisterous behavior fades into respectful tones akin to those I experienced when visiting Stonehenge.

Tucker, Rachel, and Katie then wanted to visit the Pryor Mountain Wild Horse Range in the Bighorn Canyon National Recreation Area. A long, hot drive to the middle of nowhere, with only the slimmest of chances of spotting wild horses on the thirty-one-thousand-acre preserve? Didn't sound great to me.

Rachel wouldn't back down, so I grinned and suggested we put our money—and lips!—where our mouths were. More specifically, my lips and her money.

If we spied even a few wild horses, I would bow down and kiss her feet. If not, she would buy me the most massive beer available at the closest bar, even though that would likely be miles and hours away.

We shook on it.

Wyoming dry prairie morphed into Montana sparse and dry, with random and well-spaced grasses, an occasional stand of piñon, and large rabbitbrush clumps—a harsh environment for lizards and snakes, let alone horses who drank five to ten gallons of water a day.

The conflict between cattle ranchers and proponents of wild horses on public lands will likely never end. Ranchers complain that an over-population of horses causes over-grazing, and demand mass round-ups and slaughter of these magnificent creatures. Wild horse preserves reduce these conflicts, where horse birth control is practiced by caring veterinarians, as well as wild horse auctions, where buyers can acquire a horse with exceptional spirit and historic bloodlines.

Nothing moved on the range other than us along the paved access roadway, with its parking areas and interpretive signage with photos delineating what we *might* see, if lucky.

Derived from a single Spanish stallion and abandoned mares, those "living symbols of the historic and pioneer spirit of the West" sported dorsal stripes down their backs and what looked like zebra stripes on their legs, differentiating them from their original sire.

We poured over the graphics, then lifted our hands to shade our eyes to study the miles of dusty landscape. I could taste that beer. The first, tart sip. The mellow swallow mid-mug, still icy cold but oh so satisfying.

Then . . .

About a half mile away, from the midst of a cluster of brush, a long-legged foal and its mother high-stepped into view. Ripped with muscle and in various hues, more horses followed, though all wore those telltale zebra-striped leggings. Beautiful beasts.

As the small herd foraged, Rachel pointed at her dusty toes. I'd lost our wager. She'd worn sandals that day, and as I dropped to my knees, laughter pummeled me. Despite my thirst, I joined in, even though it's not easy to pucker when you're grinning.

Farther north we passed several historical stone markers describing Colonel George Armstrong Custer's 1874 expedition. An expedition in violation of the Fort Laramie Treaty of 1868, which ceded "the country north of the North Platte River and east of the summits of the Big Horn mountains" to the Sioux Nation. Sadly it was the U.S. government's greed for Black Hills gold that triggered Custer's march into Sioux territory, which also catalyzed an invasion of white miners and settlers onto those sacred lands and prime hunting grounds. The Plains Wars between Native Americans and the United States followed.

With the discovery that my great-great-grandfather served in the Plains Wars during his time at Fort Laramie and other Forts along the western frontier, our visit to the Little Bighorn Battlefield National Monument in the Big Sky Country of Montana held special interest for me, though I knew it would be a solemn affair.

I knew my ancestor fought alongside Colonel Custer in the earlier years of the so-called Indian Campaign. Thankfully though, Captain John Rziha didn't ride with Custer and his Seventh Cavalry during that ill-fated three-pronged attack on about two thousand Lakota, Cheyenne, Arapaho, and Sioux warriors on June 25–26, 1876.

In the book *Black Elk Speaks*, I'd read:

We started and went down stream to the mouth of Muskrat Creek beyond the Santee camp. We were going to meet the second band of soldiers [Custer's detachment]. By the time we got there, they must have been fighting on the hill already, because as we rode up from the mouth of Muskrat Creek we met a Lakota with blood running out of his mouth and down over his horse's shoulders. His name was Long Elk. There were warriors ahead of us, the "fronters" who were the bravest and have the most practice at war.

When we got further up the hill, I could see the soldiers. They were off their horses, holding them by the bridles. They were ready for us and were shooting. Our people were all around the hill on every side by this time. (Neihardt, *Black Elk Speaks*, 115–16)

Custer and the 268 men in his five companies were all killed. One horse, ironically named Comanche, survived. Crazy Horse and Sitting Bull's victory was short-lived, as the news of the battle caused an uproar, an even greater response to the "Indian problem," and the eventual demise of the nomadic Plains Indian tribes.

With the "Indian problem" over and the grand herds of buffalo slaughtered to a minuscule five hundred or so, men like my great-great-grandfather became a new and different kind of problem for the U.S. government. After giving most of his later career years to the U.S. Army, it was his family now. Shockingly and painfully, many such career officers were unceremoniously thrown to the wind.

Strapped financially by post–Civil War reconstruction costs, and no longer in need of a standing army, bogus court-martial claims against high-ranking officers became the norm—an answer to avoid retirement pay. Colonel John Rziha, civil engineer for the design and mapping of fortifications across the United States during the Civil War and Indian Wars, wounded twice in battles, still carrying lead in his body from one of those wounds, was railroaded out of the army. The charges? After drinking with the enlisted men, he slapped a mule trainer for abusing his mules.

John Rziha petitioned President Grant for reinstatement of his pension but to no avail. My great-great-grandfather died from lead poisoning in 1881, alone, in a boarding house in Leadville, Colorado.

The last night of our long and dusty road trip found us in Cody, Wyoming, where we tapped our toes to fine country music at Cassie's. After a few beers we joined the local cowboys and cowgirls to swirl our partners with steps like the stomp, the shuffle, the girl turn, and the heel and toe. Though I might have felt like Fred Astaire, my wife and friends informed me that I needed more practice and that the beer did *not* improve my timing. So I shrugged, drank one more, and tried again.

37. A BLIZZARD IS COMING

When the wind blows in from the northwest in Wyoming and a single meandering line of hundreds of antelope forms, pay attention. A blizzard is coming.

It's one thing to endure a major snow event in a city or town where snowplows rumble around, ready to scrape away accumulations greater than three inches, and the grocery store and gas station are only a few miles away. There the buildings provide shelter and often block the worst of winter winds. I once had a city dweller say to me that when it snowed at the ranch it must be time to stay inside by the fire and relax!

Relax?

Eighteen miles from town and five miles to the closest neighbor. Fifty to sixty mile-per-hour winds, minus-forty-degree windchill, and hundreds of domesticated animals depending on you and your wisdom—or lack thereof.

More than once I've been caught at the ranch in exactly those conditions. With our advanced weather forecasting, we know when blizzards are on the way, so I listened carefully for "Stockman's Advisories." A day or two before any such potential event, hundreds of locals would stream into town, crowding the small supermarket and gas stations for a few extra supplies to ride out the storm.

Power outages can be rough on unprepared ranchers. Water well pumps won't work without electricity, and generators need gas, so planning ahead is critical.

Cattle will huddle together to insulate themselves from the wind, forming their own windbreak. But this can cause snowdrifts around the cattle and sometimes smother them in heavy snow, especially the calves. The immense ranches in Montana have been known to suffer the loss of hundreds of cattle during these types of storms.

Of course the worst of the storms materialize in early spring during calving season.

That particular spring day, the wind began moaning at about 7:00 a.m. By noon, snowflakes gripped my windshield on my race back from town. With the ranch and livestock solely my responsibility—no family or ranch hands at the Washtub this weekend—my mental to-do list expanded faster than my speed.

After stoking the woodstove with cured ponderosa pine logs, I tugged on my Carhartt overalls and heaviest boots before stepping out into the blinding white storm.

Too late to decide whether to move the cattle into the corral, I hoped the old mommas would guide the herd into a protected coulee or pine stand. Fortunately I'd brought the "heavies"—the mother cows that I thought would soon give birth—in the previous day. I'd also spread about a third more hay than normal, as the animals would need more energy to stay warm.

Our small herd of tough ranch horses were on their own. Shaggy with winter coats and butts to the wind, they'd bunch together, close their eyes, and fall into a sort of trance-like state to conserve energy.

Shoved by the wind and with my face and glasses icing up, every few hours, day *and* night, I staggered to the barn and corral to check the mommas and calves.

Three feet of snow and thirty-six hours later, fifteen-foot drifts reached for the crystal blue sky.

After checking the mommas yet again, I cranked up our skid steer, with its four-wheel drive and ridged tires easily capable of shoving aside the heavy snow. I quickly made it to the county road, about a half mile from our cabin, as the snow hadn't accumulated on our gravel drive.

I'd already spotted some of our cattle following the natural low snow troughs in search of hay. I pulled over to start a count and heard an engine approach. Soon, a chained-up truck pulled up—our northern neighbor. He'd been stymied by a fifteen-foot-high drift across the southern road and was trying to get into town via Fletcher Park County Road, which bisected our ranch.

We agreed there was no chance that the county would be clearing the road out our way, so after feeding our cattle, the skid steer and I visited that road-blocking drift. I'd done it a couple of years before, and now again. Two tanks of diesel later, I'd carved out a tunnel that reminded me of Trail Ridge Road in the Colorado Rockies in June, with fourteen-foot-high snow banks cut into sheer cliffs on either side of the road.

The feat also reminded me of when I was a kid on a snow day, making snow forts and tunnels, only now, some thirty years later, with bigger toys.

Blizzards in winter presaged the antics of tumbleweeds in summer, which break off from their rooted stems in the fall to fly and tumble across the prairie until stopped by an obstacle such as a barbwire fence. Such was the case that next fall as eight-foot-tall mounds of tumbleweed traffic jams draped miles and miles of our fences.

The first snow of the season would in turn be caught by the weeds, expanding without fail into Ma Nature's homegrown snow fence. The weight of the snow could then knock down or pull over our twenty miles of fence.

The arduous, weeks-long task of pitchforking the rounded weeds onto a truck, resting for a few miles as we drove to a barren preselected site, then pitchforking them out of the truck into a burn pile the size of a large house took hours and effort and muscles and patience.

The good news? We had one helluva of a marshmallow roast with flames almost fifty feet high.

38. MORE THAN FISHING

Fly fishing requires time and patience. At the ranch I rarely had enough time to enjoy a "proper" fishing expedition; my days were defined by too much to do. Managing the ranch, our share of the physical work, keeping our young boys occupied, including teaching them how to drive the truck, shoot safely, while also tubing and rafting, driving four-wheelers, and racing go-carts—I could go on and on.

We also had to cope with the occasional crisis, such as the day my older son, Shawn, lost control of his go-cart and ran into a barbwire gate at full speed. After cutting him free of the spaghetti of sharp barbs, my wife took the lead on bandaging requirements while I rebuilt the gate. When done, I checked on the family. All good. Mostly calm. I decided to seek the serenity of fishing to restore my sanity.

Gear and waders in hand, from the ridge above the river I spotted Rachel standing in the North Laramie, casting in a poetic rhythm. Sun danced across the water, and the whipping arc of fishing line emulated the most delicate of rainbows.

This early in the season, the icy snowmelt didn't encourage trout to rise, as insects weren't yet cruising above the wet boulders and tumble of water. Entranced, I inhaled deeply and sat down as a ballet of nymph fishing unfolded before me.

Crystal clear as nature intended, the ten-foot-deep pool Rachel claimed that day might hide a dozen trout—or none. It didn't matter. Not to Rachel. Not to me.

With a precision I could never claim, Rachel "presented" a nymph—a wingless fly—on the river bottom. Emulating an emerging bug, the nymph wriggled, orchestrated by Rachel's exquisite touch.

Wham! Fish on!

Controlling the weighty furious trout that had expected a tasty treat, a minute later Rachel reeled in her prize, netting a sixteen-inch brown trout. Smiling in satisfaction, I saw her nod as her gentle fingers removed the hook from the trout's mouth. Cradling the slippery beauty with both hands, she lowered the fish back into the river, releasing her catch to swim another day.

In early September that same year, 2001, the Twin Towers came down.

Piloted by Islamic terrorists, the hijacked commercial jets full of fuel crashed into that pair of iconic glass-wrapped towers. Television coverage of the horrific events rattled Americans.

Not knowing whether another attack might be imminent, Rachel, Tucker, Katie, the boys, and I retreated to the ranch where we knew we could self-sustain.

In our semicircle around the fireplace that evening, we discussed our fears, our sorrow over the day's events and lost lives, our awe of the heroes on the ground, global politics, and life's preciousness.

As architects, Rachel and I repeatedly dissected the images of the fall of those mighty towers. Thought to be invincible, the heat generated by burning jet fuel could have quickly and likely did melt the steel beam structure that then pancaked to the ground. As parents, I'm sure neither Katie nor I ever anticipated having to try to explain to our children what could be an act of war. War. Terrorists. Chaos and fear. Exhaustion finally claimed us, and we hugged each other before seeking an escape in sleep.

Without much discussion, the next morning our group—my best friends and family—decided to take a few hours' respite from the painful, ongoing broadcasts of what had been discovered thus far. Even the boys remained somber, though the hike to our favorite fishing spot, buoyed by our resolve, calmed our souls, strengthening us for whatever might lay ahead.

While one cannot truly be compared to the other, as Rachel's political prominence and clout continued to grow, so too did her fishing prowess. Her visible success as planning director stood her in such good stead that I regularly heard her name suggested as a City of Denver mayoral candidate—one supported by the current mayor.

Then it all came crashing down.

Diagnosed with a rare blood disease, we watched the light flicker from this talented woman—our friend and Tucker's love.

Medical efforts accelerated as she suffered isolation and bone marrow transplants.

Spiritual efforts followed, including a healing ceremony held for her at Confluence Park in Denver. Known as the beginning of Denver, where Natives gathered for centuries at the joining of two rivers, the South Platte and Cherry Creek, we sought and experienced a transcendent moment.

Hundreds of friends, acquaintances, and coworkers locked arms in circles within circles, surrounding Rachel. We lifted her now frail body upward, as a Native woman explained that we needed to direct our energy through one another into Rachel. We did. How we prayed.

I remembered my surprise at seeing her when Tucker brought her to the ranch that first time, our growing respect and friendship, the mystical emotions we shared at Medicine Wheel. I remembered her laughter, her knowledge, her willingness to sacrifice so much for the city she loved. I remembered watching her fish—that silken arc of a rainbow controlled with such finesse.

Tucker wept, as did so many of us, as we prayed for healing, for hope and strength for this magnificent woman, this precious life.

A single month remained for Rachel, for this bright soul I remember each time I cast a fly into a river, striving for a perfect arc between my hand and those rushing waters of life. Oh, how they rush.

39. A GOOD LIFE

It's said a blue-eyed dog can see the wind, but my Whiskey dog had brown eyes highlighted by the gold of the Incas. When he wanted to, he mimicked a mean coyote by splaying his legs wide, holding his head low, and peering at you sideways. But that dog didn't have a mean bone in his body. Nothing sly at all.

That two-year-old Aussie saw me through some tough times while a pup, and sociable could have been his middle name, at least when it came to other dogs. My dad's small border collie sassed and fussed in an effort to ride roughshod over him. Whiskey didn't mind. He didn't give one whit if Cassie wanted to play with his toys. Mostly.

Whiskey loved the ranch, whether riding in my pickup, running alongside the horses, or showing off his natural herding instincts by pushing cattle against the fence.

Most of all, he loved to chase rabbits.

With a blur of rich reddish brown, white chest, pumping legs, eighty pounds of muscle launched! He ran those brown rabbits lean. Kept them in top sprinting condition. An athlete, when Whiskey flew over a large rock, hind end high, legs tucked beneath his belly like some fancy show horse leaping over six-foot-high rails, maybe he thought *he* was a rabbit. Sometimes I'd shout at the bunnies, "Stop running and he'll stop chasing you!" But my advice always fell on fluffy, deaf ears.

A few years back, before I bought Whiskey, I chased after my own rabbits.

I burned up my days between the architectural office and the ranch, answering emails and paying taxes, fretting, planning, riding, branding, somehow finding time for skiing and biking and wondering whether we should build a riding arena or buy a new horse, jetting to Alaska, to Spain, to Berlin . . . all without pause. I didn't stop when someone shouted. Even when that shouting was my own.

I ignored my conscience, my heart, my love.

As an architect I "connect" to certain building designs, and special sites heighten that sentiment, but my soul somehow expanded when I first stepped foot onto the Devil's Washtub Ranch. A mystic or Native might claim I belonged there—that I needed this corner of the earth as it needed me. I did need it. I breathed and slept and laughed and loved with more passion and honesty on those semiarid acres encircled by twenty miles of fence than ever before.

I grew up a "white-bread" son of Colorado natives. My father worked for Chevrolet, that all-American automobile company whose advertising jingle of "baseball, hot dogs, apple pie, and Chevrolet," created by James Hartzell, could be chanted by millions. Our 1960s Sunday night family gatherings were carefully timed to include a viewing of the classic Western *Bonanza*. Our everyday values echoed those of the Cartwrights—a family whose history and core beliefs were based in God, country, family, and a reverence for the western culture, in that order.

Card-carrying Republicans and Methodists, my parents were active in the church throughout their lives. Me, not so much. I dreaded Sunday mornings as I didn't embrace or even comprehend the "business" of religion or the structured, conformist requirements of the church. I tried to concentrate on the message-laden sermons and admonitions hidden within hymns, but all too often my attention wandered as I tried in vain to decipher what often sounded like a foreign language. Nor was I moved by the need for constant offerings to maintain this religious bureaucracy.

Regardless of those Sunday morning hiccups in my upbringing, I was blessed by exemplary parents and a loving, protected youth during which I became accustomed to success. As the youngest in my class and subsequently graduating with honors from college, it naturally followed that I earned my architectural license before any of my peers. I capped that by becoming the youngest partner in a decades-old, established architectural firm.

I lived the life, blessed with a bright and beautiful wife, a fine stepson, and two lively young boys of my own. We traveled the world, nurtured our careers, and flourished.

As I grew in tenure within the architectural firm, additional responsibility landed on my shoulders, but I had an affinity for the business, and the firm benefited from my leadership and problem-solving abilities. Conversely, ranching provided intellectual *and* physical challenges, both of which I craved. Dawn might herald the optimism of morning with meadowlark song, but by dusk, that trickster, Ma Nature, often won out. Some evenings I imagined her rubbing her hands together while chortling over the myriad of obstacles hurled our way. My typical easy manner eroded more than once, yet my desire for that lifestyle and the creation of success never waned.

Then, with an excruciating and abrupt pronouncement, it all ended. After thirteen years of marriage, a terrific marriage—I thought—my wife informed me she wanted a divorce.

I fled to the ranch.

Like a cringe-worthy scene in a movie, corroboration that our relationship had failed arrived via a whispered message on the answering machine in our cabin. I must have listened to those few sentences a half dozen times before I managed to return the call of a total stranger, a woman from Washington State, a woman I'd never met, a woman who said her husband had betrayed her. With my wife.

The heartache expressed by a stranger, who'd tracked me down on our remote Wyoming property, shredded my soul. Until that moment, I'd held onto the hope that my wife and I would meet with counselors, thrash through our problems, and work everything out. My charmed life would continue.

It didn't.

Divorce lawyers, property valuations, child counselors, and the prospect of a lonely future shrouded my days and nights. Thrust into an unfamiliar one-bedroom apartment, I immediately missed the daily bustle of a family of five. I turned to my best friends and coworkers for solace and advice as I tried to understand whether this was all my fault, as my soon-to-be-ex-wife so skillfully claimed.

I lost more than forty pounds, which on my already-lean frame made daily chores a challenge not only for my frail mind but my weakening body. I no longer found joy, let alone solace, at the ranch, so I stopped making that three-hour trek unless absolutely necessary.

Spring branding loomed, and as my ex-wife coordinated that effort, I declined to attend what had once been one of my favorite days at the ranch. I couldn't embrace her peculiar belief that life at the ranch could and would go on as if nothing had happened. Something *had* happened, something I couldn't fix.

Torturous months passed. I questioned myself every day, floundered in guilt, and squandered my confidence.

Concerned about my actual sanity, my good friend and coworker Marsha suggested we travel to Santa Fe to "change the channel" on my dismal outlook. After several days of visiting art galleries, enjoying great Mexican food accompanied by lots of tequila and late-night talks circling around the meaning of life, on the last day of our trip we strolled through the Indian Market in the Central Square.

Displayed on mellow terracotta tiles, the gleam of silver and turquoise heaped atop carefully woven Navajo rugs pleased my gaze, while the smiles and dark eyes of Natives gentled my soul. I found myself drawn to one particular Native woman, she of cracked, sun-weathered skin and many decades of life, sitting cross-legged behind her display. Her deep eyes offered simple kindness.

She nodded in greeting and held up a circular, silver pendant, laser cut with a symbol I didn't recognize. "You need this now, I think," she said. "Our symbol for the sun. It means 'a good life.'"

A good life.

I donned that small piece of smooth silver, and from that moment forward, it warmed my neck as I allowed the light of the sun back into my heart. I forgave myself. I allowed the love of my friends and family to sustain my soul. I healed.

One warm spring day I drove north from Boulder with extra care, studying each landmark along the way to affix it permanently in my memory. This would be one of my final trips to the thousands of acres of Wyoming land that I cherished. We'd breathed life into that desiccated property—no, that wasn't quite right. *I'd* brought it back to life with determination and sweat and passion. Yes, my wife and ranch partners had played no small part in that effort, but they all knew, as I did, that I had borne the brunt of that effort. Now listed for sale on the Mirr Ranch Group website, the Devil's Washtub Ranch had joined a colorful collection of western ranches. It hurt. As I owned only a minority share of the ranch, I couldn't stop or even slow the sale triggered by my ex-wife, whose newfound interest in the San Juan Islands in the rainy northwest occupied her focus. She needed the money. Or wanted to put the past to bed. Probably both.

I arrived near midnight, though the full moon beat back the hours by emulating the quietest of evenings. I didn't even carry a flashlight as I walked up to the hilltop and settled, cross-legged, on a rounded granite boulder. As the screech of an owl punctuated the night's silence, I realized even the wind slumbered.

I patted the rock, smoothed, I believed, by centuries of Natives sitting and gazing as I did over the valley. Below, moonbeams danced on the waters of the North Fork of the Laramie River. Behind me, tepee rings still circled the ground. They had my back.

My new companion nudged my elbow. Whiskey, a then fifteen-week-old, chestnut-and-white Australian shepherd, watched my hands as I tugged my silver pendant out from beneath my shirt and lifted it so sun could meet moon. My face warmed as I scooted off the boulder to shout and stomp, raising dust as I danced and cried to the heavens that I was alive. That I could laugh and love and create and build. In this cathedral of nature, I didn't worry what others might think as my poor attempt at a buffalo dance sent my feet in a new direction. After close to five decades of life, visions of Natives and western spirit, of honesty and loyalty, of work and passion, sang in my heart.

I howled and spun around, stripping off my sweat-soaked shirt so moonlight would reflect back to the heavens from my tanned skin. I cried out for salvation, for love and strength . . . for happiness. I danced until, gulping for breath, I paused to lean against the granite boulder where Whiskey waited so patiently. He licked my face and I laughed, long and loud.

That autumn, as the cold winds of winter rolled across the West, the Devil's Washtub Ranch changed hands for only the fourth time. From the Natives to the Harrisons to my family, that ancient watering hole and its surrounding hills and plains, its turtles and cacti and deer and coyotes, along with the souls of all that had gone before, now belonged to a local Wheatland family, good friends of Glenn Harrison. Not quite a full circle, but tepee rings still branded that land, etched into the soil and on my heart, as clear and strong as the Navajo symbol of the sun emblazoned upon my silver pendant, the symbol of growth and life and the hope promised by every sunrise.

AFTERTHOUGHTS

With the purchase and rebuilding of the Devil's Washtub Ranch, my private dream spread its wings to soar high above me and everyone I loved. My life changed as my moral compass solidified, pointing without fail toward western culture and ethics. The mental and physical necessities *and* opportunities lured my sons outside, away from their electronic fixations. Those same opportunities immediately became a release valve for the stresses created by my architectural profession as well as those percolating within the equally dedicated souls of my wife and our ranch partners. We busted our butts creating a new hearth and home—what became a gathering place for family and friends.

I didn't expect a spiritual awakening: the discovery and acceptance of nature's raw power over humankind. The realization and recognition of our impact on the remote Wyoming landscape, compassion for wildlife that inhabits the land while struggling with the irony of raising animals humanely for food, stirred my emotions each and every day. This, seasoned with a healthy dose of respect for the environment and economics while continuing in my demanding role as partner of one of the largest architectural firms in Colorado.

The best of times. Sometimes the worst.

Was it life's coincidences or divine destiny that guided me to that specific parcel of land, the Devil's Washtub Ranch?

I believe in destiny. I believe in the ghostly force of centuries of Natives that lived so lightly upon the land. I believe my great-great-grandfather, a colonel in the U.S. Cavalry, rode across that very same land as he participated in the purge of the "Indian problem." A native of Austria, he had no ingrained knowledge or hatred of the tribes. It was simply his job in this new world, and he strived to do it well. In battered sepia photographs I see a kind man who passed his traits on to my grandmother and father—both of whom inspired me. The ethereal presence of John Rziha helped open my heart and awareness to the spiritual power of the Native tribal culture.

I learned so much, slinging hay and birthing calves. Now, so many years later, I'm grateful my decade of journals could jog my memory, as did my sons. Yes, things happened during those years that nearly broke me, that I wish I could forget, but those rare moments when a frisson of life's force claimed my soul, when I danced and stamped my feet and howled at the moon, those I claim as my own, to relive and relish forever.

Memories can be tricky, as I so often experienced at our architectural firm's board meetings. Ask each of ten partners attending the same meeting what important decisions were made, I'd receive seven different answers. I suspect my family and friends, many of whose names I've changed within this book, will remember different or additional events and details. I hope they, too, remember our joy and accomplishments, the lessons learned from even our dark moments.

We'd acquired almost three hundred cattle without a spit of knowledge about caring for them. Through the gentle and frequently cunning guidance of an old but patient ranch owner, a pretty good ranch hand was born. That would be me.

In a century-old stone ice house repurposed as my architectural studio, I continue to design structures primarily related to ranches: exquisite gates, portals to another time and place, horse barns that shelter their inhabitants while enhancing the visual landscape, and other rural structures; I've savored each and every one.

Do I miss the consuming management responsibilities I shared with the partners of oz Architecture? No. I do miss the excitement of pursuing and winning contracts for the design of complicated projects and creating award-winning architecture with my team. I also miss the camaraderie, the teamwork, and the recognition for a job well done.

Though not happy about it at the time, I am fortunate that one of our partners left oz to pursue a different dream—writing. Without Janet's guidance as CFO, and later as managing principal, I doubt oz would have accomplished all that we did, and though unintended, her decision to leave helped inspire me to again pursue my cowboy dream. This book would not have come to fruition without her wordsmithing.

Today, on a small ranch in northern Colorado with my love Alanna, we live *our* cowboy way—raising a fold of around thirty Scottish Highland cattle, long-horned, long-haired "hippie" cows—while also managing the Inn at Whiskey Belle Ranch and the nearby Forks Mercantile and Saloon.

In the predawn hours, I often rise and, with a mug of tea in hand, step out of our restored ranch home to gaze over the river valley of the North Fork of the Cache La Poudre. Early morning mist hovers above the meandering waters. Lifted by an early morning breeze, the shimmer of knee-high green grass ripples to its own rhythm, as if the Earth itself draws breath.

During these quiet moments I often think about the Natives that once roamed these western lands. Their circle of life. Their determination and honor and passion. I also ponder my awakened, changing priorities, my love. I can never walk in the boots of my great-great-grandfather or in those of the tribes whose lives were steered by nature and the seasons, and later by greed and our government, but I do walk the lands where Natives once walked. I hope I step lightly, that what I designed and built, what I created or preserved or nurtured, honors all who have gone before.

Here, where cattle graze contentedly, where hawks soar to such heights that their cries are as faint as the shadows cast by my years on the Devil's Washtub Ranch, the seasons again encircle my life. I have found peace—and my place in this world.

BIBLIOGRAPHY

"Bonanza." IMDb, accessed February 4, 2022. https://www.imdb.com/title
/tt0052451/.
"Bonanza (Theme Song)." Wikipedia, accessed February 3, 2022. https://en
.wikipedia.org/wiki/Bonanza.
Carlson, Susan. *Wyoming Historical Markers at 55mph: A Guide to Historical Markers and Monuments on Wyoming Highways*. Cheyenne WY: Beartooth Corral, 1994.
"Gene Autry's Cowboy Code." The Official Website for Gene Autry, updated September 29, 2017. https://www.geneautry.com/geneautry/geneautry
_cowboycode.html.
"Green Acres." IMDb, accessed February 3, 2022. https://www.imdb.com/title
/tt0058808/?ref_=fn_al_tt_1.
"Gunsmoke." IMDb, accessed February 3, 2022. https://www.imdb.com/title
/tt0047736/?ref_=fn_al_tt_1.
Hedron, Paul. *Fort Laramie and the Great Sioux War*. Norman: University of Oklahoma Press, 1998.
"James Hartzell." Wikipedia, accessed February 3, 2022. https://en.wikipedia.org
/wiki/James_Hartzell.
Nadeau, Remi A. *Fort Laramie and the Sioux Indians*. Englewood Cliffs NJ: Prentice-Hall, 1967.
Neihardt, John G. *Black Elk Speaks: Being the Life Story of a Holy Man of the Oglala Sioux*. Lincoln: University of Nebraska Press, 1979.
Parkman, Francis. *The Journals of Francis Parkman*. New York: Harper & Brothers Publishers, 1947.
Rand, Ayn. *The Fountainhead*. New York: Signet/New American Library, 1996.
Rand McNally. *Rand McNally Road Atlas*. Skokie IL: Rand McNally, 2000.
"Treaty of Fort Laramie (1868)." U.S. National Archives and Records Administration, accessed February 3, 2022. https://www.archives.gov/milestone
-documents/fort-laramie-treaty.
"What Are the Scout Oath and Scout Law?" Boy Scouts of America, accessed February 4, 2022. https://www.scouting.org/about/faq/question10/.
"Wile E. Coyote and the Road Runner." Wikipedia, accessed February 3, 2022.
https://en.wikipedia.org/wiki/Wile_E._Coyote_and_the_Road_Runner.

Printed in the USA
CPSIA information can be obtained
at www.ICGtesting.com
CBHW030039190524
8776CB00004B/572